"Shapiro and Borie-Holtz distinguish the reality from the rhetoric of regulatory reform by looking at past efforts through several different lenses. In clearly written prose, they review theories on what motivates regulation and initiatives for reform, present empirical analysis of reform efforts in the states, and supplement their findings with in-depth case studies and interviews. Anyone interested in understanding the motivations and effects of regulatory reform, regardless of their views on its merits, will benefit from reading this book."

—Susan E. Dudley, Director,
The George Washington University Regulatory Studies Center

"This important book provocatively challenges the conventional wisdom of regulatory reform, making the case that administrative procedures do little to affect the timing or outcomes of government rulemaking. Shapiro and Borie-Holtz convincingly explain why politicians nevertheless act as if procedure matters, revealing why regulatory reform remains a popular but controversial item on state and federal policy agendas."

—Cary Coglianese, Edward B. Shils Professor of Law
and Professor of Political Science, University of Pennsylvania

I0025159

The Politics of Regulatory Reform

Regulation has become a front-page topic recently, often referenced by politicians in conjunction with the current state of the U.S. economy. Yet despite regulation's increased presence in current politics and media, *The Politics of Regulatory Reform* argues that the regulatory process and its influence on the economy is misunderstood by the general public as well as by many politicians.

In this book, two experienced regulation scholars confront questions relevant to both academic scholars and those with a general interest in ascertaining the effects and importance of regulation. How does regulation impact the economy? What roles do politicians play in making regulatory decisions? Why do politicians enact laws that require regulations and then try to hamper agencies' abilities to issue those same regulations? The authors answer these questions and untangle the misperceptions behind regulation by using an area of regulatory policy that has been underutilized until now. Rather than focusing on the federal government, Shapiro and Borie-Holtz have gathered a unique dataset on the regulatory process and output in the United States. They use state-specific data from twenty-eight states, as well as a series of case studies on regulatory reform, to question widespread impressions and ideas about the regulatory process.

The result is an incisive and comprehensive study of the relationship between politics and regulation that also encompasses the effects of regulation and the reasons why regulatory reforms are enacted.

Stuart Shapiro is Associate Professor and Director of the Public Policy Program at the Bloustein School of Planning and Public Policy, Rutgers University. Professor Shapiro's research focuses on the regulatory process and regulatory reform, including the role of cost-benefit analysis, public participation, and e-rulemaking. He has also done research on the regulatory process in the states. Prior to becoming a professor, he was a desk officer and manager in the Office of Information and Regulatory Affairs at the Office of Management and Budget.

Debra Borie-Holtz is an instructor at the Bloustein School and a senior research analyst at the Center for Women and Work. Debra's research interests include state legislative leadership and policy formation, regulations, women in government, and survey methodology. Prior to receiving her doctorate, Debra held a Presidential appointment as an agency director during the Clinton Administration and served as New Jersey Assistant Secretary of State during the Florio Administration.

Routledge Research in Public Administration and Public Policy

The Politics of Regulatory Reform

Stuart Shapiro and Debra Borie-Holtz

Routledge
Taylor & Francis Group

NEW YORK AND LONDON

First published 2013
by Routledge
711 Third Avenue, New York, NY 10017

Simultaneously published in the UK
by Routledge
2 Park Square, Milton Park, Abingdon, Oxfordshire OX14 4RN

First issued in paperback 2015

*Routledge is an imprint of the Taylor & Francis Group,
an informa business*

Library of Congress Cataloging-in-Publication Data

Shapiro, Stuart.
   The politics of regulatory reform / Stuart Shapiro, Debra Borie-Holtz.
      pages cm. — (Routledge research in public administration and public
policy ; 6)
   1. Trade regulation—United States. 2. United States—Economic
conditions. I. Borie-Holtz, Debra. II. Title.
   HD3616.U47S378 2013
   352.80973—dc23
   2013018737

ISBN 13: 978-1-138-94471-8 (pbk)
ISBN 13: 978-0-415-64246-0 (hbk)

Typeset in Sabon
by Apex CoVantage, LLC

To Anne for everything and to Noah and Seth for making me so happy by just being you.

To Harry and Joan for loving and encouraging me at every step of my life, to Bethany and Maddie for bringing me so much joy, and to John, whose love and enduring support have been my constant companions throughout our lives together.

Contents

Tables

Figures

Acknowledgements

At the end of a long journey, it is always important to reflect on those who have shared the experience with you. In the case of our pursuit to explore the regulatory regimes of the states, it is impossible to forget those who journeyed with us, as this book would not have been possible without their contributions along the way.

At every step of the research, we had the support of a group of graduate and undergraduate students whose enthusiasm for research piqued their curiosity and fed their enthusiasm for the project despite the tedium that is often associated with data collection and coding. From the Bloustein School of Planning and Public Policy, our team of data coders included Savannah Barnett, Eden DeChavez, Harini Kidambi, Ashish Matthew, Sukhjinder Singh, and Candace Valente. Their work helping us collect and code thousands of regulations is a large part of the reason we were able to shed some light on regulatory reform in the states. In our earliest days on the project, before we contemplated the book, we also received the assistance of two graduate students, Michele Sloan and Christina Spellman. We are grateful to all.

We also want to thank a very dedicated group of students who helped us field our survey of Midwestern Business Leaders. We say dedicated because they volunteered their time over a winter semester break to help us build a sample frame of elite business executives so that we could be in the field in January. This team included two of our own, Kellie Palomba and Saundra Session, as well as two students from Gettysburg College, Jonathan Faul and Bethany Holtz. Kellie, Saundra, and Bethany continued with the survey project over the spring semester by pretesting the instruments in multiple modes, updating contact lists, coding data, and even surveying respondents over the phone. A random probability survey of business elites presents unique methodological challenges, but the team's contributions and attention to detail made this area of our research possible.

Three other students deserve special acknowledgement. They were the research assistants who persevered the longest with us, and as a result, they made the most significant contributions to the project. They are Michael Wong, Joseph Rua, and Juan Rodriguez. Michael was our first undergraduate to join the team. He became our senior research assistant who not only conducted top-tier research for us but then went on to serve as a mentor and supervisor for all of our research assistants. Michael also took the lead on the survey design and, along with Joseph Rua, was largely responsible for researching and drafting the literature reviews, which extended over many theoretical frames. In addition to writing literature reviews, Joseph took the lead on researching the legislative history for our two case studies in Pennsylvania and North Carolina. He also helped us track down our interviewees for Chapter Seven. Of course, Michael and Joseph also logged many hours coding state regulations. Juan Rodriguez aided the project by collecting and coding the regulations we used in our longitudinal study of the five Midwestern states. After logging hundreds of hours coding state rules, Juan along with Michael and Joseph committed to stay with the project to its conclusion. All three worked tirelessly to meet whatever task or deadline we gave them. Perhaps there is no greater contribution to a research study than meeting deadlines and ensuring your work is accurate. All three met the high standards we set for the project and we are grateful for and proud of their contributions.

Much of this research would not have been possible without the willing participation of so many stakeholders involved in the regulatory process who offered us their time to be interviewed. We appreciate their insights into the process and their sensitivity to our deadlines. Their perspectives have helped to shed new light onto the regulatory process in the states.

It goes without saying that within an academic community, there is a wide supply of support, advice, and encouragement you can derive from your colleagues. We are grateful to those at the Bloustein School who encouraged our work along the way, from hallway conversations to more formal consultations. Of note, we would like to thank Cliff Zukin for reviewing our Midwest Business Leaders' survey instrument and offering valuable methodological suggestions, Anne Gowen for proofreading Chapter 1, Tamara Swedberg for serving as our technology guru—helping us create regulatory flowcharts to customizing landing pages for our web-based survey—and David Redlawsk at the Eagleton Center for Public Interest Polling for donating his time overseeing the telephone survey we fielded at the Center. Of course, many others lent a hand from time to time by assisting our students with computer, phone, and office access so the research could actually take place when it needed to. In the end, none of our requests for assistance went unanswered and we are extremely appreciative for this support. We also want to thank two discussants at the Association for Public Policy Analysis and Management conference who provided us with helpful comments to our earliest chapter drafts: Jim Marone at Brown University and Eric Patashnik at the University of Virginia. Anonymous peer reviewers of individual chapters, the proposed manuscript, and the final book all provided helpful comments and made this a more thoughtful and well-rounded work.

Above all, a special thanks to our families who may not necessarily share our passion for studying regulatory reform but who nonetheless made many sacrifices that enabled us to conduct the research and draft, edit, and prepare the final manuscript. This book could not have been written without their unwavering support, patience, and encouragement.

1 The Mystery of Regulatory Reform

As long as there have been regulations, there have been attempts to influence the way those regulations are written. Regulations are generally developed by the unelected "fourth branch" of government, agencies that report to either the legislative or executive branch. Because these regulations have impacts on special interests and on the public, and because interests (special or public) cannot influence regulatory output directly through the electoral mechanism, questions of how to imbue the regulatory process with the accountability associated with the legislative process go back at least to the creation of the first regulatory agencies (Eisner 2000).

Often these attempts to influence agency regulatory decisions take the shape of requiring agencies to follow certain procedures when they issue regulations. As the regulatory state has grown, so has the prevalence of these procedures. At the federal level, the first major effort to proceduralize the regulatory process was the Administrative Procedure Act (APA) in 1946.[1] In the sixty-seven years since the passage of the APA, Congress has increasingly turned to procedures as a means of attempting to influence agency decisions (Epstein and O'Halloran 1999). In the 112th Congress more than a dozen such bills were considered.

Attempts to use procedures to influence regulatory agencies are not limited to the legislature. Presidents and governors have often used procedures to more closely supervise the agencies that ostensibly report to them. By requiring executive review of regulations or requiring agencies to perform an analysis of their regulations, executives hope to overcome the perceived weaknesses associated with the appointment power as a means of overseeing agency decisions (Nathan 1983).

Collectively these procedures are generally described as "regulatory reforms." Such reforms are often promoted as having other purposes in addition to attempting to increase the accountability of regulatory agencies. Requirements for public participation in regulatory decisions increase stakeholder investment in regulations, and in doing so, hopefully increase support for such decisions (Davis 1969). Requirements for cost-benefit analysis hope to ensure that agencies make decisions that are more economically sound (Hahn 2000). Requirements for regulatory negotiation hope to reduce litigation over regulations (Harter 1982). Requirements that regulations sunset after a prescribed period of time are intended to force agencies to revisit the wisdom of their decisions. Deadlines for regulations are intended to overcome bureaucratic torpor (Gersen and O'Connell 2008).

There has been considerable scholarly attention paid to regulatory reforms, or "procedural controls" as they are often called in the political science literature. Huber and Shipan (2002) write, "[s]cholars seem to agree that the use of procedural rather than policy details represents the most important way in which Congressional majorities use legislation to influence bureaucratic autonomy." But there is a mystery associated with regulatory reforms. Much of the empirical study of the effect of regulatory reforms shows limited and ambiguous effects. Given the proliferation of regulatory reforms—and academic attempts to understand them—one would expect them to have significant policy implications. Why do politicians continue to enact them despite the limited evidence that they work? Are they motivated by the nobler aims in the previous paragraphs or is there a more self-serving impulse at work?

This book is an attempt to unravel this mystery. To begin our investigation, it is first critical to understand theories of the regulatory state. These theories attempt to explain the motivation of agencies that write regulations and of the political actors that attempt to influence those regulatory decisions. Such theories are numerous (Croley 1998), and regulatory reforms have a role in each of them. This chapter reviews the various theories of the regulatory state and where regulatory reforms fit into them. After discussing regulatory reform from a theoretical perspective, we move on to discuss empirical examinations of regulatory reforms, and show how these studies largely argue that the reforms have failed to live up to the promise that proponents have made for them.

This book adds critical new data to the debates on regulatory reform by examining these reforms in the fifty states. By first reaffirming findings that regulatory reforms achieve more symbolically than substantively, we heighten the fundamental mystery of regulatory reforms described above. We then use state data to try and understand why politicians turn to regulatory reform, and we argue that we should be much more skeptical of politicians trumpeting regulatory reforms as solutions to management of the regulatory state. It turns out that the politics of regulatory reform are much more about politicians serving their self-interests than improvements to regulatory decision-making. And it appears that regulatory reform can be much better explained by theories of political behavior than by theories of the regulatory state.

1.1 THEORIES OF THE REGULATORY STATE

Croley (1998) lays out four theories of the administrative (or regulatory) state, and contends that understanding them is critical to understanding the procedures that political overseers require agency bureaucrats to follow when promulgating regulations. Further, he argues that regulatory procedures should be understood through the lens of these theories. These theories have been developed by various scholars attempting to explain political and bureaucratic behavior. Each of them assumes that particular groups are empowered by the regulatory process and therefore favor certain types of procedures. Regulatory procedures, according to Croley, are methods that politicians use to advance the interests of certain groups (including possibly the broader public interest).

The first theory described by Croley is the highly influential public choice theory. Articulated more than forty years ago by Stigler (1971) and Peltzman (1976), public choice theorists argue that powerful interests dominate the competition over regulatory choices.[2] Legislators seeking reelection create administrative procedures that will give these powerful interests preferred access to bureaucratic decision-makers and are rewarded by these interests with their support. Bureaucrats, as independent decision-makers, are largely omitted from the model, with the tacit assumption that once the decision-making environment is established, agency decisions will serve the powerful interests that hold sway in the legislative process.

Becker (1983) offered a modified version of the public choice theory, which Croley describes as the neopluralist school. Like their pluralist predecessors, neopluralists view the regulatory process as a competition between interest groups and analogize this competition to the way the market works. Unlike public choice scholars, neopluralists do not view this competition as inevitably dominated by powerful interests. Croley argues that if the neopluralist vision of the administrative state is correct, then procedures should reflect enhanced interest group competition. As an example of a regulatory procedure that advances interest group competition, Whisnant and DeWitt Cherry (1996) argue that one of the primary goals of regulatory analysis is to enhance political debate, or to "increase the politicization of rulemaking." In their view, analysis helps make agency decisions clearer to the interests affected by them.

The final two theories articulated by Croley are the civic republican and deliberative democracy models. Each of these models finds more of a place for the public interest than the public choice or neopluralist models. The deliberative democracy vision of the administrative state views participation by all interested parties as central to good decision-making (Gutmann and Thompson 2004; Staszewski 2012). These scholars argue that agency decision-making has the potential to be deliberative in nature and the process should facilitate this deliberation. This vision has found support in early advocates of participation (Davis 1969), supporters of regulatory negotiation (Harter 1982), and more current reformers who have held out the hope that electronic rulemaking will lead to greater participation and better regulatory decisions (Johnson 1998).

The civic republican model allows for agency bureaucrats to implement their vision of the public good (Reich 1985). Their ability to do so rests upon the amount of slack they are given to make decisions out of the view of political overseers. The role of bureaucratic slack comes up in numerous debates over regulatory reforms (Levine 2007). Supporters of bureaucratic expertise argue that high slack will lead to better outcomes than decisions made by agencies influenced by politics (Morrison 1986). Those who fear that slack enables bureaucratic rent seeking, and behaviors like budget maximization (Niskanen 1971), or zealous pursuit of mission (Downs 1967), worry about high slack for agency experts. A focus on slack is an important aspect of the debate on regulatory reforms, as many of the reforms are intended to curb agency discretion.

Rossi (1997) also catalogs several models of the administrative state. Of the three models that Rossi describes, his expertocratic model is the most distinct from the ones described in Croley's typology (although there are some similarities to the civic republican model). While Rossi acknowledges a role for deliberation, he contends that for deliberation to be useful it must be informed by expertise. Supporters of an expertocratic vision believe that agencies populated with experts are best positioned to use their expertise to ensure that deliberative decisions lead to good policies, and that administrative procedures should be designed to insulate experts from special interests.

The theories of the regulatory state all have a place for regulatory reforms. Some, particularly the public choice model, also include a place for self-interested politicians. But even the public choice model assumes that regulations, and by extension regulatory reforms, deliver favors to particular constituencies. These theories give little explanation for enactment of measures of limited effectiveness. We believe that in order to understand the political motivations for regulatory reforms, theories of political self-interest must be front and center.

One of the most important of such theories is contained in Mayhew's (2004) landmark study of legislative behavior, which described the behavior of legislators motivated by reelection. Among his descriptions of legislative behavior are "position seeking," in which legislators advance arguments in order to appear effective; "credit claiming," which describes Congressional attempts to provide services for constituents; and advertising by legislators to publicize their actions. The first two of these may have particular relevance to the legislative (and executive) decision to enact regulatory reforms.

The "credit seeking" behavior was given more detail in Fiorina's (1989) study of the relationship between Congress and the bureaucracy. Fiorina argued that Congress and the bureaucracy have a symbiotic relationship. Congress creates bureaucracies that impose costs on citizens (either directly or by not disbursing benefits quickly enough). Citizens complain to their Congressional representatives about the bureaucracy, and then when the representative fixes the particular problem, (s)he has won the electoral loyalty of the complaining citizen. Congress thus creates a need for its own services by establishing bureaucratic agencies.

While Fiorina focused on the delivery of benefits (such as food stamps) rather than regulation, regulation can fit in this framework as well. Congress requires bureaucracies to write regulations by passing vague laws that require specification. When the details in the regulations inevitably displease a constituency, legislators have another opportunity to deliver a service to voters. In this context, regulatory reforms could be seen either as a way of delivering that service ("you don't like the EPA, well now here is a way for you to influence their decisions") or by creating another institution that can be subjected to legislative oversight (like a regulatory review office). In this view, regulatory reforms are not intended to achieve particular policy aims, but rather to serve as mechanisms for credit-seeking politicians to exploit future dissatisfaction with regulatory decisions, and to facilitate the occasional change in an agency regulation.

Modeling Regulatory Reforms

Beginning in the 1980s, political scientists began to mathematically model legislative decisions to impose regulatory reforms (or procedural controls) on bureaucratic decision-makers. These models illustrate the underlying models of the regulatory state discussed above, but they also introduce some new elements to the discussion. These political scientists described these controls as attempts by the legislative coalition that put them in place (the "enacting coalition") to control decisions that they have delegated to the executive branch. Calvert and Weingast (1982) framed the problem by describing the difficulties that Congress faces in overseeing federal agencies and their lackluster motivation to do the extensive work associated with conducting such oversight.

McCubbins and Schwartz (1984), in contrast, argued that oversight was not as difficult as others had maintained. They saw procedural controls as a way of facilitating "fire alarm" oversight by legislators whereby legislators respond to constituents when they point out problems with agency decisions. McCubbins and Schwartz (1984) argued that this was a much more efficient way of overseeing agency decisions than "police-patrol" oversight, which involves regular hearings on agency behavior. In this view, regulatory reforms actually play a key role in helping Congress oversee agencies.

McCubbins, Noll, and Weingast (or McNollgast, as they are commonly referred to) took this a step further and argued that procedural controls were attempts by enacting coalitions to overcome the problem of legislative oversight through "deck-stacking." According to McNollgast (1987, 1989), enacting coalitions used procedural controls to stack the deck so that bureaucrats implementing statutes (including via regulation) would face the same pressures that the legislature had faced when passing the statutes. These controls would increase the probability that the substantive decisions reached by agency officials would mirror the decisions that legislators would have made.

The McNollgast model inspired numerous expansions. Hill and Brazier (1991) explain that structure and process requirements for implementing rules and regulations help control bureaucracies by mitigating the informational advantage administrative agencies have over legislators and other third parties. This is done by building delay into the process so that coalition members (Congressional committee chairs, the President, etc.) can monitor decision-making. More importantly, private groups whose interests are represented will have time to notify Congress regarding any issues or transgressions associated with the agency policy decision. Lupia and McCubbins (1994) explain that institutional designs (such as regulatory reforms) are ways for legislators to overcome their informational disadvantages compared to agency bureaucrats.

McNollgast and those who expanded on their work are not without their critics. In particular, Horn and Shepsle (1989) point out that while procedural controls or regulatory reforms may help enacting coalitions defend against bureaucratic drift (the tendency for agencies to make decisions differently than legislators), they may exacerbate coalitional drift. Coalitional drift refers to the fact that the political coalition in power changes over time and newer coalitions may not have the same preferences as older ones. Procedural controls often give future coalitions additional ways of implementing their policy preferences and, in doing so, could lead to policy choices contrary to the desires of the enacting coalitions.[3] In other words, procedural controls may do the exact opposite of ensuring that the will of the enacting coalition is followed.

Spence (1997) accused McNollgast and subsequent proponents of deck stacking of "modeling away the delegation" problem.

> Positive theorists do this by assuming away the importance of substantive policy foresight to politicians' efforts to influence subsequent agency decisions. Quantitative empiricists do this by choosing as their dependent variable agency implementation of established policies, rather than agency policy making itself. While both are driven to this result by their own separate methodological imperatives (and a commendable preference for scientific rigor), the result is the same. Neither group of models is sufficiently rich or generalizable to challenge the notion that agencies act with a great deal of autonomy when exercising most delegated policy-making authority. (199)

According to Spence, neither group has shown that regulatory reforms (or similar procedures) are effective.

Other Perspectives on the Role of Regulatory Reforms

While much of the political science literature on regulatory reforms focuses on the relationship between legislators and agencies, executive control of agencies is also important. In a number of articles, Moe (1987, 1990) argued that political scientists had focused on Congress, and inappropriately ignored the executive branch. Legal scholars, by contrast, have engaged in considerable evaluation of executive oversight and have debated at great length the wisdom of presidential review of agency regulations. Critics such as Morrison (1986) and Schultz-Bressman and Vandenbergh (2006) argue that presidential review undermines the statutory goals for regulatory agencies, and substitutes presidential preferences for agency expertise and deliberation (see also Staszewski 2012).

Executive review also has its supporters. Most prominently, Justice Kagan argued that presidential review enhances agency accountability because the President is the only official elected by the entire American public (Kagan 2001). Kagan also argues that coordination among executive branch agencies is improved through executive review, and bureaucratic torpor is best overcome through careful executive oversight. At the federal level, review of agency regulations by the Office of Information and Regulatory Affairs (OIRA) has been long supported by those who argue that it brings additional perspectives to agency decisions, and enhances political control of agencies (Blumstein 2001; Katzen 2007).

Legal scholars have also made another critical contribution to the debate over regulatory reform. McGarity (1992) first articulated the theory that regulatory procedures, coupled with "hard-look" judicial review of agency regulations, has ossified the regulatory process. Regulatory procedures have raised the costs of agency rulemaking to such an extent that agencies were avoiding issuing regulations and turning to other less burdensome means of setting policy that were free of such constraints (such as enforcement actions or guidance documents). McGarity leaves unanswered the question of whether crippling the regulatory process is the goal of those implementing regulatory reform, but others have made this claim explicit (Vladeck and McGarity 1995), dubbing the phenomena "paralysis by analysis."

Tying It Together

The debate over regulatory reform has many strains, as can be seen from this brief summary. Many of these strains have overlapping aspects. Regulatory reforms may enable the influence of powerful special interests as posited by public choice theory. They may do so by ossifying the regulatory process, making it hard for agencies to regulate these interests. The civic republican school of public-interested regulators being given the oversight slack to make decisions that benefit the public good mirrors to some degree the expertocratic view that the administrative process allows agency experts to apply their expertise.

The debates about regulatory reforms take place along numerous dimensions. Pluralists and deliberative democrats debate the wisdom of widespread participation. Political scientists and legal scholars argue over whether enacting coalitions can (and should) constrain later coalitions of politicians and whether Congress or the President should reign supreme in regulatory decisions. Public choice theorists argue that powerful interests dominate the regulatory process and regulatory reforms abet their domination, while neopluralists see regulatory reforms as a way of using interest group competition to arrive at beneficial results.

But what actually happens to bureaucratic decision-making when regulatory reforms are implemented? Some of the outcomes predicted by theories of the regulatory state and the effect of regulatory reforms are easier to test than others. The argument that the regulatory process has become ossified is particularly easy to test by examining the relationship between regulatory procedures and the time it takes to complete a rule or the volume of rulemaking. Arguments about regulatory reforms as a means of facilitating political control such as those put forward by McNollgast (1987) are harder to evaluate. They involve discerning whether decisions by agencies favor a particular outcome because of the procedures, or because of one of many other factors. Still, evidence that procedures have little effect and that regulations closely mirror the preferences of existing political coalitions would indicate a failure of regulatory reforms to enforce enacting coalition preferences. And if there is such a failure, it raises the question of why enacting coalitions have chosen to pursue ineffective measures such as regulatory reforms.

Most difficult to evaluate is the question of who is empowered by regulatory reforms. Do regulatory procedures serve the interests primarily of powerful interests, as public choice scholars predict that they will? Or do they in fact empower a broader group of affected parties, like pluralists and deliberative democrats argue that some reforms will do? Are they a tool to help politicians deliver services to constituents (thereby helping politicians' reelection prospects), as Fiorina characterized government bureaucracies? Or is curbing the discretion of unaccountable agency experts even possible through procedural methods?

1.2 EMPIRICAL STUDIES

Empirical examination of the regulatory process was once considered a backwater in political science and legal studies. Coglianese (2002) called for greater empirical analysis of administrative law questions, reflecting a dearth of such studies since the blossoming of the regulatory state in the 1960s and 1970s. The past decade, however, has seen an abundance of examinations of regulatory process questions, although, as the discussion below reflects, many questions remain unanswered. One reason that answering many of these questions is a challenge is because many studies focus on the federal government, where generation of a large sample size is challenging. Only more recently have a few scholars begun to use the fifty states as a source of data on the role of regulatory reform in regulatory decision-making. Here we very briefly review the empirical studies of the differing types of regulatory reforms on the federal and state levels.

Public Participation

The area of the regulatory process that has received the most attention is the oldest regulatory reform, the notice-and-comment process. While participation requirements go as far back as regulations, notice-and-comment in its modern form was created by the Administrative Procedure Act in 1946. Agencies are required to propose their regulations publicly, provide time for public comment, and then respond to the comments in the preamble to their final rules. Courts have required the responses by agencies to be non-dismissive, but agencies are in no way bound to adopt the suggestions of commenters.

Studies of agency responsiveness to comments have found that agencies are likely to respond to comments submitted by the public only in certain limited circumstances. Golden (1998) found that agencies were not likely to modify their proposals except when commenters with opposing perspectives agreed on an issue. West (2004) studied forty rulemakings and concluded that the primary role of the public comment process was to highlight issues for political overseers (confirming, to some degree, the McNollgast view), but even this was limited in its impact (see also Balla 1998; Yackee 2006). Yackee and Yackee (2006) found that business had an upper hand in the public comment process, which gives support to the public choice school.

One form of participation that has garnered a fair amount of academic attention is regulatory negotiation. Reg-neg, as it is often known, requires agencies to sit down with the parties affected by a regulation and negotiate the contents of the rule. Considerable dispute exists about the effectiveness of reg-neg. Advocates of the process such as Harter (1982, 2001) argue that the process saves time and reduces litigation over regulation. Coglianese (1997), in an empirical assessment, examines a series of regulatory negotiations and finds that the purported benefits of the process have not materialized.

Legislative and Executive Review

Because of the Supreme Court decision *INS v Chadha*,[4] which overturned the one-house Congressional veto, legislative review of agency regulatory decisions is nearly nonexistent on the federal level. The Congressional Review Act was passed in 1995[5] as a replacement, but because it requires a presidential signature, and a President is very unlikely to agree to veto a regulation issued by his own Administration, the CRA has been used only one time. That instance—a regulation promulgated at the end of one Administration with a succeeding Congress and President of the opposing party—will very rarely be repeated (Finkel and Sullivan 2011).

Executive review at the federal level is justifiably the subject of much more attention. Schultz-Bressman and Vandenbergh (2006) argue that review by the President's staff (including but not limited to the Office of Management and Budget (OMB)) has been experienced by the Environmental Protection Agency (EPA) employees as interference in their pursuit of policy goals. This agrees with earlier criticisms of OIRA review as biased in an antiregulatory direction (Morrison 1986). Most of the criticisms of executive oversight, however, are based on individual case studies.

Justice Kagan (2001), drawing on her experience at the Domestic Policy Council under President Clinton, argued that presidential control helped in coordination of executive branch activities, and to overcome bureaucratic pathologies such as devotion to mission or torpor. Demuth (2011), a former OIRA Administrator, argues that OIRA's influence has been overstated and that its impact has been minimal. The most detailed empirical study was by Croley (2003), who examined data on OMB review and concluded, "The White House has clearly used rulemaking review to put its own mark on agency rules increasingly often over the past two decades . . . it appears to have done so in a fairly if imperfectly translucent, open and evenhanded way" (883). Croley's conclusion fits the pluralist model of decision-making and supports the view of proponents of executive review.

Regulatory Analysis

Closely tied (at least on the federal level) to executive review is the requirement that federal agencies engage in a form of cost-benefit analysis for a certain subsection of their regulations.[6] Many agency regulatory decisions are also subject to requirements that the agencies examine the economic impact of their decisions on particular constituencies such as small business. Opponents of cost-benefit analysis have argued that it has weakened regulations, although such arguments are usually theoretical rather than empirical (Ackerman and Heinzerling 2004). Wagner (2012) uses an EPA analysis to argue that Regulatory Impact Analyses (RIAs) are used to justify regulations more often than influence the policy decisions embedded in the regulations. This comports with an analysis by Shapiro (2005) that argues that the requirement for cost-benefit analysis, because it is tied to executive review, has always taken a backseat to the political needs of the President (see also Arbuckle 2011).

Shapiro and Morrall (2012) analyzed a series of rules and their underlying analyses, and found no appreciable relationship between the extent of the information provided in the analysis and the net benefits of the rule. On the other hand, they find that political factors such as the salience of the rule, and whether it was a midnight regulation, did correlate with net benefits. This finding (and the others above on cost-benefit analysis) cast doubt about the ability of regulatory analysis to have the effects that many proponents expect.

Deadlines and Delay

The use of deadlines to constrain bureaucratic discretion has received much less attention than other types of regulatory reforms. The one significant analysis is by Gersen and O'Connell (2008). They found that deadlines do shorten the amount of time it takes to complete a rule for an agency but also that deadlines lead to reductions in public participation and that agencies frequently miss deadlines—thereby calling into question their effectiveness.

The McGarity (1992) argument that regulatory reforms and judicial review have combined to cripple agency regulators and deter them from issuing regulations has recently received increased empirical attention. McGarity himself relied on a case study of the National Highway Traffic and Safety Administration (NHTSA) that indicated that the agency had moved away from rulemaking and instead was relying upon recalls of cars to implement policy (Mashaw and Harfst 1990). Other occasional case studies and accounts in the popular press have cited examples of regulations that have taken years to complete.[7]

Arrayed against the ossification argument have been nonacademic studies of the numbers of rules, and academic empirical analysis. In the former category are annual studies by the Competitive Enterprise Institute that show that the number of regulations issued by the federal government has been steady or even increased despite the increased proceduralization of the regulatory process (Crews 2012). Kerwin and Furlong (1992) analyzed EPA regulations and found that the time to complete a regulation varied considerably and unpredictably. More recently, Coglianese (2009) cast doubt on the original analysis of NHTSA, and Johnson (2008) argued that ossification has not been a problem at the EPA. In the most detailed analysis of the time it takes agencies to complete a rule, Yackee and Yackee (2010) show that for a dataset composed of rules across agencies, those regulations that had to go through certain procedures (such as OIRA review) actually were completed more quickly than rules that did not.

Studies of the States

The foregoing studies all examine regulation on the federal level. There are good reasons that scholars have focused on the federal government. Federal regulations have extremely large impacts, with some reaching costs of billions of dollars. The federal government has largely been at the forefront of reforming the regulatory process, with ideas filtering down to the states rather than bubbling up from them. And finally, with the Federal Register and Unified Agenda online for more than a decade (and public comments available through regulations.gov), and regular reports to Congress on the impacts of regulation, data on the federal regulatory process has been far more plentiful than data in the states.

But in the past several years, a number of studies of state regulations have begun to surface. With a much greater variety of regulatory processes and political climates, the states are potentially fertile ground for researchers attempting to better understand the effect of regulatory procedures. And while federal regulations are individually more significant than any state regulation, collectively states regulate 20 percent of the U.S. economy (Teske 2004), arguing for better understanding of how state regulations are created.

Several of the studies echo the results on the federal level, which cast doubt about the influence of regulatory reforms on regulatory decisions. Whisnant and De Cherry (1996) looked at the use of cost-benefit analysis in North Carolina and raised questions about its application there. They speculated that limited capacity and commitment restricted the ability of states to use analysis to influence regulations. Shapiro (2002) found that procedural controls had little impact on the development of child care licensing standards in eight states.

On the other hand, Teske (2004) argued, "much of the evidence here, consistent with the findings of other studies of state regulation, demonstrates that government regulatory institutions do shape state regulatory policy outcomes in important ways." (29) This is to some degree supported by several works relying upon surveys of state officials about the *perceived* influence of the political branches of government. Perceived influence is of course distinct from actual influence, but it is still informative. In a 2004 article, Woods found that agency officials perceived gubernatorial oversight as more effective than legislative review. He followed this up in a 2005 article showing that stronger political branches led to decreased perceptions of interest group influence. Woods also used the survey data to conclude that provisions broadening access and notification to the rulemaking process increased the perception of influence of outside actors, particularly the courts and interest groups. Also using survey data, Dometrius (2002) looked at gubernatorial oversight and concluded that oversight (or at least what bureaucrats perceived as oversight) was effective when the governor had higher approval ratings.

Legislative influence has been of particular interest on the state level, perhaps because meaningful legislative review is absent on the federal level. Teske (2004) says, "Legislatures play an important role when they are directly making regulatory policy themselves or when they are overseeing regulatory policies that are largely developed (via rule-making) and implemented by state bureaucratic agencies" (198). The literature shows mixed results for the impact of legislative review. An article n the Harvard Law Review ("Oversight and Insight" 2007) examined legislative review in Connecticut and Alaska and showed that it did result in changes to agency regulations. Ethridge (1984) examined legislative review in three states, and found that stricter rules were more likely to be reviewed (but did not analyze the effect on the reviewed regulations). Finally, Hahn (2000) examined both economic analysis and legislative review. He found many requirements but little evidence that the requirements had improved regulatory outcomes.

Political Influence Outside of Procedures

As discussed above, the movement by legislators and governors toward procedures to oversee agency decisions arose in light of the perceived ineffectiveness of other means of oversight (Calvert and Weingast 1982). Over the past two decades, however, there have been increasingly sophisticated studies that have examined the power of executives and legislatures to oversee bureaucratic agencies. Largely these have found that bureaucrats are more responsive to political leadership than had been previously thought.

Two leaders in this field have been Dan Wood and Richard Waterman, who have looked at political oversight in several contexts. In a 1991 study, they found that bureaucracies are more responsive "at certain times in the cycle of U.S. politics," particularly after changes in power in one of the branches of government. They also found that the budgetary process and the power of executives (with approval of the legislature) to appoint agency leaders were important means of control over agencies. The findings were echoed in another study (Wood and Waterman 1993), when they found, "The budget and political appointment variables explain most of the variation in EPA enforcements; they also produce the fastest responses" (524).

Balla (2000b) used responsiveness at the Health Care Financing Administration (HCFA) to test political control. He found that responsiveness varied with the type of political interaction and that it was difficult to make generalizations (see also Balla 2000a). In a study of the Federal Reserve, Krause (1994) found that decisions by the members of the Fed's Board of Governors often reflect the preferences of the Presidents who appointed them.

If the appropriations process and the power to appoint agency leadership are effective means of political control of the bureaucracy and if regulatory reforms themselves are not terribly effective, it leads us to a compelling question. Why regulatory reform?

1.3 THE MYSTERY OF REGULATORY REFORM

In the 112th Congress, more than a dozen bills were introduced to modify the federal regulatory process. A new Model State Administrative Procedure Act was issued in 2010 (Levin 2011), and many states have enacted major new requirements for agencies writing regulations over the past decade (Schwartz 2010). They have done so despite disagreement among scholars about the wisdom of regulatory reform and limited empirical evidence that regulatory reforms have any significant effects on regulations. Why do states continue to enact regulatory reform despite these questions? This is the mystery of regulatory reform.

In this book we attempt to use new data to assess the role of regulatory reform and the motivation of those who enact it. In particular we use data from the "laboratories of democracy," the fifty states. At the federal level, there is one executive, one legislature, and one set of procedures that most agencies must follow. To gain variation, an examination must either look over a long period of time or across policy areas (e.g., O'Connell 2008; Shapiro 2007; Yackee and Yackee 2010). Each of these approaches introduces additional variables that must be controlled for. Changing political and economic conditions can confound studies over time, and the politics of different policy areas are a challenge for studies that include multiple policy areas.

Examining the fifty states allows us to more closely look at the effects and rationale for regulatory reform in varying procedural environments. Our dataset is described in more detail in Chapter Two, but it includes data on both regulatory procedures across states and the volume of rulemaking across a subsection of states. Throughout the book we supplement analyses of these data with case studies of individual states to flesh out the results of the data analysis.

We are primarily interested in the answers to two sets of questions. The first set involves analyzing the effect of regulatory reforms. Do reforms allow enacting coalitions to control policy in the manner hypothesized by McNollgast (1987)? Do they empower particular constituencies, and in doing so lead to more stringent regulations or more deregulation? Do they cripple or ossify the regulatory process, resulting in regulatory agencies turning away from regulation as a policy-making tool? Or are they largely ineffective?

The second set of questions grows from the answers to the first. As we will describe in Chapters Two and Three, and as the studies above show, the effect of regulatory reform on policy is limited. We then turn to the mystery of why politicians sitting in legislatures and in governors' offices enact regulatory reforms? The theories of the regulatory state listed above imply that regulatory reforms serve special interests, the public interest, or bureaucratic experts. But if regulatory reforms have little effect, then they serve none of these groups, and why enact them?

One possibility is that regulations are so important in their effects on the national or state economies that even limited success is worthwhile. Certainly much of the recent rhetoric on regulation gives the impression that regulatory impacts are large. Does regulation actually have the effects that its critics maintain (i.e., it damages the economy)? The mixed evidence is discussed in Chapter Four. If the actual effects of regulation on the economy are limited, then what about the perceived effects? And what other motivations do political actors have for enacting regulatory reforms? Can we use other information about the motivations of state political actors to understand their decision to enact regulatory reforms? In the absence of this are we left with seeing regulatory reforms largely as some form of credit seeking? Are they merely institutions that can be exploited on an ad hoc basis by political overseers to respond to fire alarms set off by constituents? And if so, what are the implications for the enacting of future reforms?

This book proceeds as follows. In Chapters Two and Three we focus on the impact of regulatory reforms. In addition to describing our data, we examine the relationship between the extent of regulatory procedures and regulatory volume in twenty-eight states. We discover that, contrary to some expectations, more procedures do not mean fewer regulations. In fact it is hard to discern any relationship between regulatory reform and regulation. Instead, political factors such as control of the legislature and (to a lesser degree) the governor's office appear to have the bigger impacts on agency decisions to issue regulations. We hypothesize that the biggest factors driving regulatory policy are the many laws passed that require regulatory action by agencies. We flesh out these conclusions with a case study of regulatory reform in New Jersey in Chapter Three. The results of the New Jersey case study confirm the questions about the role of regulatory reform, and add further questions about the role of political leaders in overseeing agency decisions.

This sets up the mystery that the rest of the book is intended to address: Why is regulatory reform an attractive option for legislators and governors? Chapters Four and Five take a detour into examining the actual and perceived effect of regulations. Are regulations having such a large impact (as political rhetoric might lead us to believe) that regulatory reform is a desperate attempt to solve a real and significant economic problem? In Chapter Four we review the literature on the economic effect of regulations, particularly of environmental regulations. Chapter Five presents a study of five Midwestern states, examining their environmental regulation over the course of a decade and trying to discern changes in the state economies. We find limited evidence of economic impacts but a significant perception among Midwestern business owners that there are too many regulations; it ranks as of one of the three most serious concerns facing business leaders today.

The limited actual impact and significant perceived impact of regulations begin to give a clue about the answer to the mystery of regulatory reform. Politicians interested in reelection must respond to perceptions. So the first part of the answer is that regulatory reform is a way to react to businesses' perception and say, "we are doing something about regulation" without really doing anything to upset those who support regulation. This is consistent with Mayhew's (2004) explanation of legislative behavior (which extends to executives as well) as "position taking."

But this still leaves questions. If the effects of regulation are smaller than believed, but the perceived effects are large, is regulatory reform a way to satisfy powerful interests, as expected by public choice theorists? Or does the limited impact of regulatory reforms indicate that politicians are balancing interests, satisfying industry with symbolic changes while doing little to actually curb regulations supported by many interests (as pluralists might argue)? Or are these regulatory reforms a symbolic tip of the hat to a deliberative democracy vision of the regulatory state, even if they don't meaningfully increase participation? Finally, do regulatory reforms give the public the illusion that politicians are systematically overseeing bureaucrats while behaving as Fiorina predicted and creating institutions that they can exploit on limited occasions and that otherwise have little effect on regulations? This last option is the one we believe to be the second motivation for regulatory reforms. Chapters Six and Seven explain why we've come to this conclusion and also reinforce the argument that regulatory reforms are a form of "position taking."

In Chapter Six we use our data on regulatory reforms across all fifty states to examine the question of why certain states adopt them and others do not. We draw on literature on influences on state policy to test hypotheses about possible influences on the decision to enact regulatory reforms. Looking at variables like political party control, legislative professionalism, and diffusion of ideas across state lines, we attempt to fit the desire for regulatory reform into both the theoretical frameworks of the regulatory state and other policy-making theories. Few of these theories seem to fit the adoption of regulatory reform. However there is some indication that regulatory reform is a tool used by politicians to create institutions that can be exploited by political actors in particular cases.

We examine this further in Chapter Seven with two states where regulatory reform has been rampant over the past two decades. In Pennsylvania and North Carolina, every type of regulatory reform we examine is present. In examining the motives of legislators and governors who institute and then use these reforms, we find that politicians enacting regulatory reforms are often trying to deal with economic conditions over which they have little control.

In a climate where some politicians have blamed regulation for the poor economy, there is a need to enact changes that politicians can claim will affect regulation. There is, however, little support for changing the laws that require regulation or for repealing specific regulations. As an alternative to amending or repealing laws, regulatory reform allows some politicians to claim credit for addressing the problem of regulation and also to create a means for intervening in particular regulatory decisions on behalf of constituents.

We attempt to summarize the findings from these varying studies in Chapter Eight. What should political actors confronting decisions on the enactment of regulatory reforms do? To borrow a term from one of the most popular requirements placed on regulating agencies: Do the benefits justify the costs for regulatory reforms? If, as we argue, the benefits and costs are both much lower than perceived, what are the implications for regulatory reform? We advocate a high degree of skepticism when politicians argue that regulatory reform will result in significant changes in policy.

2 Do Regulatory Reforms Influence Regulations?

Regulatory reform is the label given to efforts by politicians to influence agency decisions on regulations via modifications to the regulatory process, as we described in Chapter One. Academics often call regulatory reforms "procedural controls." The most popular ones require that the executive or legislative branch review regulations before their issuance, require agencies to conduct an economic analysis or an analysis of the impact of the regulation on a particular community, and mandate that the agency solicit participation and specify how the agency must respond to participation. Agencies are also sometimes given deadlines to issue a regulation or required to periodically review their regulations.

A great deal of energy has been spent implementing regulatory reforms over the past few decades. At the federal level, statutes such as the Administrative Procedure Act, the Regulatory Flexibility Act, and the Unfunded Mandates Reform Act (and many others) all made changes to the regulatory process. Many more proposals for changes to the regulatory process have been debated but not enacted. A recent report by the Institute for Policy Integrity documents a similar level of activity at the state level (Schwartz 2010).

Why do politicians implement regulatory reforms? We examine that question in more detail in the chapters to come. But at its simplest level, the answer must have something to do with a desire to influence regulations. So, do regulatory reforms influence regulations? This question is of critical importance. If regulations are a problem (as conservatives like to claim) or vital (as liberals tend to claim), then democratic influence on their content is desirable. Regulatory reforms are one of the primary means by which politicians attempt to exercise democratic influence on agency regulatory decision-making (Mendelson 2011).

On the other hand, regulatory reforms also have a cost. Going through executive or legislative review takes time. So does doing an economic analysis. This means it will take longer to write regulations, and in theory (if there is no separate funding for agencies to undertake these tasks) more procedures should mean fewer regulations. Indeed, critics of regulatory reforms including academics, politicians, and even agency bureaucrats subject to the reforms have voiced this criticism of regulatory reform (McGarity 1992).

In the previous chapter, we outlined various theories of the regulatory state. These theories attempt to explain the motivation behind regulations (serving powerful interests, serving the public, applying expertise) and in doing so can also provide an explanation for regulatory reforms (Croley 1998). A first step in understanding why politicians turn to regulatory reform as a policy option is to understand whether regulatory reforms actually work. If they do work as intended, then they may provide validity for one or more of theories described in Chapter One. If they do not work, then further exploration of the role of regulations and of regulatory reform is needed.

This chapter is an attempt to use state level data to expand upon federal studies examining whether regulatory reforms influence regulatory decisions. We find, in agreement with many of the federal studies of regulatory reforms, such reforms have limited effects. The procedural provision that appears to have the greatest effect on regulatory output is a requirement that agencies complete their rulemaking within a prescribed period of time (see Table 2.3). This requirement led to fewer rules being promulgated. Regulatory deadlines have received less attention from scholars and politicians than many other reforms (Gersen and O'Connell 2008). Executive review appears to deter rulemaking, but only when the governor is a Republican.

What did seem to matter was politics, but not equally from all branches. States with Democratic legislatures promulgated an average of 475 rules, while states with split legislatures promulgated an average of 360 rules; states with Republican legislatures only adopted 203 rules on average. The relationship continues when one eliminates budgetary and administrative regulations. There appears to be no real difference in the number of rules based upon the party of the governor. These partisan variables, as well as the procedural variables examined, are analyzed in detail in Section 2.3 of this chapter. Our findings support those who argue that existing coalitions hold power that earlier enacting coalitions are helpless to cabin through procedures. But it also raises questions about why politicians continually return to procedures as a means of controlling agency decisions.

This chapter proceeds as follows. In the next section, we briefly review the history of regulatory reform. In Section 2.2, we describe our data collection process, the variables studied, and provide some definitions. In Section 2.3, we present our analysis. Section 2.4 is a discussion of the results and offers conclusions.

2.1 REGULATORY REFORM AND REGULATORY OUTPUT

The regulatory process is more than 100 years old, and for more than 100 years there have been attempts to reform it. As executive agencies and independent commissions gained power in the first part of the twentieth century, concerns grew about the democratic accountability of decisions made by unelected officials. The Administrative Procedure Act (APA) was passed in

1946,[1] creating the notice and comment process in an attempt to add a layer of transparency and accountability to the regulatory process (Davis 1969).

After the creation of many more regulatory agencies in the 1960s, the modern era of social regulation bloomed in the 1970s. As a reaction to this vast increase in regulation, businesses and other opponents of regulation began to call for ways to reform the regulatory process. The hope was that changes to the process would result in changes to the substance of regulation and decreases in the number of regulations coming out of agencies (Eisner 2000).

The regulatory reform movement that began with the passage of the Regulatory Flexibility Act and the Paperwork Reduction Act by Congress in 1980 continues today. The 112th Congress considered more than a dozen bills that would change the regulatory process, most notably the Regulations from the Executive In Need of Scrutiny (REINS) Act[2] and the Regulatory Accountability Act.[3]

Over this period, the regulatory process has been amended many times. Table 2.1 shows a partial list of the changes to the federal regulatory process.

State governments have also continually revised their regulatory processes, particularly picking up the pace in the 2000s (Schwartz 2010).

What has the effect of all of this regulatory reform been? As described in Chapter One, political scientists have argued that regulatory reforms are used by legislators to influence agency decision-making. In this way, the reforms are a way of ensuring adherence to the will of the legislative (and executive) coalition that enacted them (the "enacting coalition"). Their advocates have claimed that these reforms have reduced the regulatory burden on small

Table 2.1 Federal Regulatory Reforms

Name	Year	Intent
Regulatory Flexibility Act	1980	Relieve regulatory burden on small businesses
Paperwork Reduction Act	1980	Reduce paperwork burden
Executive Order 12291 (later replaced by E.O. 12866)	1981	Require presidential review and cost-benefit analysis of regulations
Executive Order 12475	1985	Require regulatory planning by agencies
Unfunded Mandates Reform Act	1995	Require agencies to analyze regulatory impacts on state and local governments
Congressional Review Act	1995	Simplify process by which Congress can veto a regulation
Information Quality Act	2000	Allow challenges to information disseminated by government (including to support regulations)
Regulatory Peer Review	2003	Require peer review of information used to support regulations

businesses,[4] increased the net benefits of regulations (Portney 1984), and promoted participation in governance (Davis 1969).

Critics have argued that these reforms have made it harder for agencies to issue regulations. McGarity (1992) popularized the term the "ossification of the regulatory process." He argued that the various requirements put in place by Congress and by the President have raised the cost of rulemaking to such a degree that agencies would abandon regulation as a policy-making option. This criticism finds its way into every debate on regulatory reform, often assuming the moniker "paralysis by analysis."

The empirical literature that we reviewed in Chapter One on the effect of procedural controls on the federal level is at best indeterminate. Researchers have found that agencies often try to make their key regulatory decisions before procedural controls kick in (West 2009). While each of these mechanisms (notice and comment, economic analysis, and executive review) can be shown to have an impact in particular circumstances, the literature on the federal level appears to indicate that they do not have systematic or significant effects on agency decision-making. None of these procedures appear to ensure that the will of the enacting coalition that put the procedure in place will be followed.

The rhetoric around regulatory reform suggests its importance is huge. Supporters (those wary about regulation) argue that reforms can stem the tide of agency overreach. Opponents (supporters of a strong regulatory regime) argue that it has destroyed the ability of agencies to write regulations. Woods' surveys (2004, 2005) show that agency personnel also hold the perception that regulatory reforms have an impact on the decisions they make. The limited academic evidence that looks at actual regulatory decisions, however, suggests that the impact of procedures on policy is small. Our intent in this chapter is to use the "laboratories of democracy" to examine cross-state variation in regulatory reform. If regulatory reforms such as executive review, legislative review, and economic analysis have an impact on regulation, that impact should manifest itself in the volume of rulemaking.

In this chapter we examine the effect of regulatory procedures on regulatory output. Regulatory output is not a perfect proxy for the impact of regulations. However, there are a number of characteristics that make it a useful dependent variable. First, a central claim of those opposing regulatory reforms is that such reforms make it harder to regulate (McGarity 1992). If the cost of writing a regulation has risen for agencies, then it follows that fewer regulations will be produced (unless agency resources are increasing, but those cases are few and far between). Therefore, examining the effect of regulatory reforms on regulatory output provides a direct test of the argument that reform dampens output.

As for the other side of the argument—whether reforms lead to more effective regulations—the connection between output and impact is less strong but still viable. Critics of regulation often cite the number of regulations and conflate it with regulatory stringency in the public's mind and in political rhetoric (Crews 2012). Moreover, most regulations do impose a constraint on private action, and hence the volume of regulatory activity has often served as a proxy for regulatory burden (Crews 2012).[5] In addition, we find a statistically significant reverse correlation (–0.37) between the number of regulations in a state and the "regulatory freedom" in that state as measured by Sorens and Ruger (2009). This indicates that having more regulations does correlate with regulatory stringency and hence has some validity as a measure of stringency. The relationship between the volume of rulemaking and the stringency is unlikely to be perfect, but it also strikes us that these two variables are likely to be related.[6]

If there is no relationship between the presence of procedures and the level of regulatory output, then do other factors in the political environment explain regulatory output in the states? Horn and Shepsle (1989) argued that coalitions that put procedures in place to control bureaucratic drift leave themselves open to changes in who holds the political reins or "coalitional drift." Are existing coalitions able to enforce their will over state agencies regardless of the procedural environment in which they operate? In the next section, we describe our data before moving on to an examination of the hypotheses that procedures and politics affect the number of rules issued by a state.

2.2 OUR DATA

Dependent Variable—How Many Rules?

We collected data on all rules issued in 2007 from the twenty-eight states[7] that put data about final regulations online.[8] Although not a full examination of all fifty states, we tested for discernible bias and believe the states we looked at provide a representative sample of rulemaking activity in 2007. The final rules we studied were collected from states in all four census regions of the country: nine states from the Midwest, five states from the Northeast, and seven states each from the South and the West regions. Within each region, the Census Bureau further stratifies states into divisions, with two divisions in each region with the exception of the South, which has three regions. The data was collected from states in all nine census divisions. Thus, while we do not have California, Texas, and Florida in our database, the states we did examine are a representative sample of the nation as a whole.

The states are also representative politically. The state legislature was governed by Democrats in eleven of the states in 2007, by Republicans in eight, and was split between the two parties in nine of the states in our dataset. It was more lopsided in the governor's mansion, where twenty-one of the twenty-eight states were governed by Democrats (the 2006 elections swept Democrats into statehouses nationwide). Eleven of the states voted for John Kerry for President in 2004 and seventeen of them voted for George W. Bush.

Finally, as for our key independent variable—the presence of procedures to control agency regulatory actions—our states represent an excellent cross section. As described below in the discussions of the three key regulatory reforms; executive control of rulemaking, legislative control of rulemaking, and economic analysis requirements, all three variables have scores across our entire spectrum for the stringency of the control.[9]

While we report the total number of rules (8961 rules in the twenty-eight states), it does not serve well as a dependent variable for state regulatory activity. States use rulemaking in different ways. For example, most states use rulemaking to administer their Medicaid program, with some states issuing more than fifty "Medicaid rules" in 2007. Some states do not use rulemaking for Medicaid, meaning that the total number of rules means different things in different states.

To deal with this problem, we borrowed a concept from the Office of Information and Regulatory Affairs. We separated out rules with a real economic impact on society from "budgetary" rules that govern programs, like Medicaid, that merely disburse funds. We also eliminated rules that set the hunting season for various animals, because the extent to which states use rulemaking for this purpose varies considerably between states. Finally, we also eliminated purely administrative regulations that set rules for the state government, not the public. This left us with a variable we called "economic rules," rules that impose an economic constraint on private action, which totaled 5356 rules for the twenty-eight states. The total for each state is in Table 2.2 along with data on the number of laws passed in 2005 and 2006. This reflects a more adequate measure of the regulatory activity in each state in 2007.

We note that our "economic rules" variable incorporates what scholars of regulation call "social regulations" (regulations designed to curb externalities or information asymmetries in order to improve public health) as well as "economic regulations" (regulations that restrict prices or quantities of goods or services). Both of these types of regulations restrict private behavior and hence have an economic effect.

While the procedures that we examine affect all regulations issued in a state, there is reason to believe that they will act differently in different policy areas. The politics surrounding an issue vary by policy area and therefore the role of regulatory reforms and of political actors may vary (Wilson 1980). The very nature of certain procedures may lead to different impacts in different policy areas. Cost-benefit analysis is harder or easier depending on the nature of the question being analyzed. Deadlines are more relevant when the policy question being answered is more complicated.

There were five policy areas that were common to the vast majority of states we examined. These policy areas also made up a significant portion of the total number of economic regulations that we used as our aggregate dependent variable. The five policy areas are environment, transportation, agriculture, insurance and banking, and education. For each of the analyses conducted in Section 2.3, we report the results in aggregate and then note if there are any differences in the five policy areas. If there is no mention of the specific policy areas, then the results were the same as the aggregate results.

Table 2.2 Law and Rules per State in 2007

	2005 Chapter Laws	2006 Chapter Laws	2005–06 Chapter Laws	2007 Total Rules	2007 Economic Impact Rules
Arizona	334	395	729	145	93
Arkansas	2325	39	2364	298	131
Delaware	228	237	465	191	140
Idaho	402	875	1277	229	145
Illinois	263	434	697	381	183
Indiana	248	194	442	218	85
Iowa	181	188	369	463	254
Kansas	223	231	454	113	62
Louisiana	583	911	1494	542	219
Maine	320	224	544	418	246
Michigan	340	682	1022	64	58
Minnesota	169	170	339	72	36
Missouri	199	170	369	184	126
Montana	611	0	611	160	70
Nevada	511	0	511	674	562
New Hampshire	298	328	626	324	197
New Jersey	384	103	487	474	371
New Mexico	354	112	466	546	319
New York	231	348	579	681	514
North Carolina	463	264	727	152	110
Oklahoma	481	814	1295	508	274
Pennsylvania	136	229	365	77	44
South Dakota	284	268	552	78	45
Tennessee	506	516	1022	281	172
Virginia	951	947	1898	367	237
Washington	519	372	891	993	484
Wisconsin	87	404	491	134	99
Wyoming	255	124	379	194	80
TOTAL	11,886	9579	21,465	8961	5356

Independent Variables: Procedural Controls

We collected data on the regulatory process for each state, including data on executive and legislative review, requirements for impact analyses, rulemaking deadlines, and sunset provisions.[10] During our data collection process, the Institute for Policy Integrity (IPI) issued a detailed report on the role of executive and legislative review, impact analysis, and sunset provisions in the states. The IPI report was based on data collection and interviews in all fifty states. For each procedural requirement that the IPI studied, they compared the legal requirements with the practice in each state (Schwartz 2010). This data was far more extensive than anything previously available and became the primary source for our data on these regulatory reforms.

For legislative review, executive review, and impact analysis, we developed ten-point scales for the extent of the reach of each procedure in each state in our database. The ten-point scale for each of these variables is detailed in Appendix 1. The scores were based on the descriptions in the IPI report. Several scales on legislative review had been developed (prior to the issuance of the IPI report). Our scale has a correlation coefficient of 0.62 with Gerber, Maestas, and Dometrius' (2005) scale and a correlation coefficient of 0.63 with the scale developed by Grady and Simon (2002). These correlation coefficients indicate that our legislative review scale possesses external validity.

Agreement with the executive review scale developed by Grady and Simon (2002) was less strong, with a correlation coefficient of 0.47. This value is still statistically significant (using a two tailed t-test at the 5 percent confidence level). Further, detail on executive review before the IPI report was harder to access because much of it is informal (as opposed to legislative review, which is often in statute), so we believe our data (really, IPI's data) on executive review is the best available. We also collected dichotomous data on whether or not states require a written response to agency comments,[11] whether agencies sunset their rules, and whether they place a deadline on rulemaking.

Independent Variables: Politics and Demographics

We collected data on political variables in each state in an effort to control for differences in political preferences for regulation. First, we measured for differences in political culture, which were defined by the general election vote for President in the 2004 cycle. We also collected data on the partisan control of the governor's office and both chambers of the legislature in 2007; we further noted those instances where control of the legislature was divided. With the exception of two states, New Jersey and Virginia, state legislatures elect their members in even-numbered years, therefore the 2007 legislature was the first year of a new session for most states. Given the likelihood that some rules finalized in 2007 resulted from lawmaking in the prior session, we also took a look at partisan control in 2006. While individual members may have changed, the partisan makeup of the states changed only slightly in 2007 as compared to 2006. In six states the partisan control shifted from a single party control to split control;[12] only New Hampshire shifted from Republican control in 2006 to Democratic control in 2007.

2.3 ANALYSIS

The central question we evaluated is whether the presence of regulatory procedures influences the level of rulemaking. We are also interested in the impact of existing coalitions on rulemaking, so we compare our political variables with the volume of regulatory activity. This section is broken up by the categories of independent variables. First we discuss the role of procedures in regulatory output and then the role of politics.

With a sample size of twenty-eight states, our ability to use multiple independent variables is limited. After the comparisons of individual variables, a third subsection below includes some simple multivariable analyses. Given the limited number of correlations found in the first two sections, the likelihood that significant relationships would be found in a multivariate analysis is limited. Still, multivariate analysis would strengthen our understanding of these relationships and we strongly recommend further work in this area.

Administrative Procedures

The twenty-eight states we examined provide considerable variation in their use of regulatory procedures, which allows for an examination of their effects that extends beyond what scholars have studied previously. In this section we describe the interaction between six types of procedures and rulemaking output. As described above, three of these variables are constructed as a ten-point scale: executive review, legislative review, and economic analysis. The other three variables are yes/no variables: sunset requirements, deadlines for finalizing rules, and the requirement that agencies respond to comments.

Executive Review

As described in the appendix, the ten-point scale for the executive review variable is made up of four components. These four are whether the review is required or optional, whether it is binding or nonbinding, who conducts the review (the governor's office or another office in the executive branch), and the criteria for the review. The average score for the twenty-eight states is 5.5 and the median score is a six. There was considerable clustering near the ends of the scale, with ten states receiving a zero and six states receiving a ten.

The correlation coefficient for the total number of rules, the number of economic rules, and the number of rules in each of the five policy areas with the level of executive review was negative but small and statistically insignificant[13] (–0.19 and –0.16, respectively). The negative correlation is expected, as executive review is criticized as one of the procedures that often deters rulemaking. The small magnitude and statistical insignificance of the relationship seems to indicate that by itself, executive review does not dissuade agencies from engaging in rulemaking.

However, if one examines the six states that scored a ten in the executive review variable,[14] a possible relationship emerges. The average number of economic rules in these six states was ninety-eight rules, but the average for the other twenty-two states was 216 rules (breaking out the ten states that scored zero showed no relationship with level of rulemaking). This difference was statistically significant[15] using a one-sided t-test and may show that in its most extreme forms, executive review has an impact on the level of rulemaking. However we should note that of these six states, three had Republican governors and two of the other three had legislatures controlled by Republicans. This may indicate that existing coalition control provides a more compelling explanation for rulemaking volume.

Legislative Review

Like the executive review variable, the ten-point scale for the legislative review variable has several components. Review is considered more stringent if it is mandatory instead of voluntary, if legislatures actually have veto authority (without requiring a governor's signature), and if there are fewer restrictions on the legal grounds for legislative disapproval of a regulation. The average review score is 5.5 and the median is five. There are fewer extreme values for this variable than for the executive review variable, with only three states with values of zero[16] and two states with a "perfect" ten.[17]

The strength of legislative review has no correlation with the volume of rulemaking in the state. Correlation coefficients were close to zero for both total rules and economic rules. This was also true for each of the five policy areas we examined. Six out of thirteen states with a legislative review score below the median issued more than the median number of rules in 2007, while six out of fifteen states at or above the median level of legislative review issued more than the median number of rules.

Impact Analysis

The final of our three variables with a ten-point scale was the stringency of impact analysis requirements in the states. States received a higher score based on the number of rules for which analysis was required (intermediate scores were given for states that had a threshold for requiring analysis), for requiring analysis of all costs and benefits instead of just government impacts, and for the type and extent of review of the analysis. The mean and median scores were both six, and three states scored a zero[18] while four states scored a ten.[19]

Like legislative review, a requirement that agencies analyze economic impacts, shows no relationship with the volume of rulemaking. The correlation coefficients for total number of rules, rules with an economic effect, and rules in all five policy areas are all nearly zero, and the level of rulemaking for states with below and above the median analysis score are virtually identical. It appears that both impact analysis and legislative review have no relationship with the number of rules that agencies promulgate.

Other Procedures

All of the states have some form of notice and comment. Only ten of the twenty-eight states in the study, however, require that agencies actually publish responses to agency comments. We hypothesized that requiring an agency response might deter rulemaking but actually found no statistically significant relationship. For both the total number of rules, and economic rules, more rules were promulgated in the ten states with required agency responses than in the eighteen states that allowed agencies to publish final rules without a response. The difference is small and not statistically significant, however.

A number of states require agencies to finalize their rules within a certain period of time after the close of the public comment period. Sixteen states (out of our twenty-eight) have such deadlines, and the deadlines vary from seventy-five days after the end of public comments to two years after the comment period is concluded. Theoretically such deadlines should cut down on the number of final rules, because agencies may not be able to finalize all of their proposals within the prescribed time limits.

Indeed, this is one procedural control that works just as predicted. States with rulemaking deadlines promulgated an average of 233 rules and 139 economic rules. States without a deadline promulgated an average of 432 rules and 265 economic rules. The differences are statistically significant for both variables at the 5 percent level. While all five policy areas showed higher levels of rulemaking in states without deadlines, the relationship was statistically significant in education and agriculture, but not in the other three areas. Still, this is the clearest impact of any administrative procedure. Placing a deadline on the completion of agency rulemaking following a proposed rule results in fewer final rules.

The final procedure we examined was a sunset provision. States with sunset provisions issue more rules than states without them. However, this may be because states with sunset provisions have to undertake rulemaking to re-promulgate sunsetting rules. This alone could drive up the level of rulemaking in these states (we were unable to separate out new rules from re-promulgated rules, so we can merely hypothesize that this is what is happening here).

Overall, looking at the relationship between a single regulatory reform and the number of economic regulations adopted in these twenty-eight states, only the requirement of a deadline for completion showed a moderate to strong and statistically significant relationship.

Political Variables

If enacting coalitions can have only very limited effects on future agency actions through procedural controls, what about existing coalitions? We

Table 2.3 Correlations among Economic Rules and Regulatory Reforms

Number of Economic Rules (n=28 states)		
Oversight & Analysis	Correlation	p Value
Executive Review	−0.256	0.189
Legislative Review	0.100	0.613
Fiscal Oversight	−0.136	0.491
Time Deadlines	−0.465*	0.013
Sunset Provision	0.181	0.357
Response to Comments	0.295	0.128
Total Scale	−0.181	−0.181

Note: p value is a two-tailed test.

compared the party control of the governor's office and the legislature to the level of regulatory output. The clearest impact was control of the legislature. We collected data on legislative control in both 2006 and 2007 because, conceivably, agencies could be engaging in rulemaking to implement statutes passed either by the current legislature or the previous one. Democratic control of the legislature correlates with rulemaking volume regardless of the session of the legislature, as shown in Table 2.4.

This speaks volumes to the issue of existing coalition power in state rulemaking. Democratic control of state legislatures likely compels rulemaking from agencies more often than Republican control. Note, we are not measuring whether the substance of the rules comports with the intent of the legislature. Even without this data, however, the level of rulemaking output is highly suggestive of existing coalition control.

The difference between Democratic and Republican control is statistically significant (using a one-sided t-test for a difference between the mean number of rules in Democratic states and Republican states) for legislative control in both 2006 and 2007, and for both total number of rules and for economic rules. If one includes the cases where control of the legislature was

Table 2.4 Legislative Control and Regulatory Output

2006 Party Control of Legislature	2006 Average No of Rules	2006 Average No of Economic Rules	2007 Party Control of Legislature	2006 Average No. of Rules	2007 Average No. of Economic Rules
D (8)	475	258	D (11)	424	231
S (7)	360	250	S (9)	323	219
R (13)	203	119	R (8)	173	104

split with those where Republicans were in control (in effect arguing that control of one house of the legislature is enough to prevent the passage of statutes that require regulation), the difference in total rules between Democratic-controlled legislatures (in 2006 and 2007) and all other legislatures is statistically significant (again using a one-sided t-test), but not the difference in economic rules.

All five policy areas exhibited higher levels of regulation under Democratic-controlled legislatures (both 2006 and 2007) than in Republican-controlled legislatures. The difference between states with Democratic and Republican legislatures was statistically significant for environment, education, and insurance/banking, but not for transportation or agriculture. If one includes the split legislatures on either side, the statistical significance disappears in all policy areas.

Why might legislative control be so important in determining regulatory volume? Regulations have their genesis in laws that authorize them. Laws are, of course, the creation of legislatures. These results indicate that the control of these legislatures is a significant determinant of regulatory volume. Democratic legislatures are more likely to pass regulatory laws and hence more likely to produce high volumes of regulation. This is important because if regulation is largely due to laws, then regulatory reform (even if it works) is an inefficient way to reduce regulation. Politicians wanting to eliminate regulations should repeal the laws that authorize them.

The degree to which legislators are prescriptive about legislative intent or include implementation parameters in the enabling statute likely determines both the scope and number of regulations that follow. Clear and precise laws require agencies to write rules that are proposed and adopted shortly following enactment. We categorize such rules as "mandatory regulations."

Alternatively, "discretionary regulations" are derived from many sources. A regulation may be used as an instrument to address changes that occur in the regulated community (or changes in our understanding of threats to public health) following the passage of the original law. Such changes may require additional clarification or modifications of existing mandatory regulations. Vaguely drafted laws trigger a series of rulemaking procedures as bureaucrats try to gauge the original intent of the law and find the right balance. Regulators may also be forced to arbitrate disputes left unresolved during the legislative debate because the provisions were deemed too politically charged or sensitive, in which case the legislative decisions are deferred to the executive branch.

All of this serves to produce discretionary regulations that transpire over a period of years following the enactment of a law. At the federal level, the Environmental Protection Agency continues to produce regulations under the Clean Air Act passed in 1970 and last amended in 1990. Similarly, the Department of Health and Human Services will be issuing regulations under the Affordable Care Act for decades. While those less familiar with the administrative state may believe that laws are drafted with clear and precise standards, those that study American government realize that this is far from reality in most cases. There is a vast literature on the subject of administrative discretion produced by administrative law scholars and political scientists (see for example, Calvert and Weingast 1982; Davis 1969; Fiorina 1989).

If legislators are more prolific lawmakers in some states as compared to others, then the number of regulations that are adopted may be higher in those state capitals. This possibility is important to examine as it may help explain why party control of the legislature makes a difference in regulatory volume, and why regulatory procedures are less effective in determining regulatory volume. No regulatory procedure can mitigate against the passage of a law that demands an ensuing regulatory action. If mandatory regulations make up a large portion of overall regulation, then that would further substantiate the fruitless nature of regulatory reform. What happens if we look at the relationship between the number of laws passed in a state and the number of regulations?

When we run correlations between the number of laws (shown in Table 5.1) and the number of regulations in our twenty-eight states, there is no significant relationship. This is true regardless of whether we use the number of laws passed one year or two years prior to the study year of 2007 for regulations. There are a number of reasons that this type of analysis is limited, however.

Agencies may take years to implement statutes (even clearly written statutes) with regulations. Some statutes have deadlines for regulatory action, but many others do not. Because of the volume of laws in the twenty-eight states, we were unable to differentiate between substantive laws and those that are purely administrative or ceremonial in nature. Nor did we distinguish between substantive laws that require regulation for implementation and those that do not. Because of these problems, the lack of a relationship between the number of laws and the number of regulations is not surprising and should not take away from the fact that states with Democratic legislatures produce more regulations. We return to this subject in Chapter Five, where we take advantage of a smaller sample of states to reexamine this relationship in more detail.

Interestingly, party control of the governor's office has little relationship to the level of rulemaking output. The twenty-one states with Democratic governors in 2007 issued an average of 310 rules (with 184 economic rules) compared to 350 (212 economic rules) for the seven states with Republican governors. The difference is not statistically significant.

Combinations of Variables

One could come up with a large number of hypotheses about how combinations of the variables described above could affect rulemaking output. While our sample size is too small to run regressions with large numbers of independent variables and get meaningful results, we can look in detail at combinations of two or three variables. Even restricting ourselves to such combinations leaves many possibilities, however. We decided to focus on two types of combinations. First, we examined whether procedural controls operating together deterred rulemaking, a claim often voiced by opponents of such procedures (Vladeck and McGarity 1995). Second, we examined party control of the legislature in combination with legislative review, and party control of the governor's mansion with executive review, to see if we could shed any light on the particular impacts of these controls.

Combinations of Procedures

The simplest way to examine the impact of the three main procedures studied (legislative review, executive review, and economic analysis) is to add them together. Since all three procedural variables were given a zero-to-ten scale, adding them together weights them equally. The correlation between the number of rules (total and economic) and the combined score for the three procedures is not statistically significant, casting further doubts on the argument that procedures deter rulemaking.

We then examined the various combinations of the three controls to see if any particular combination shows an impact on rulemaking. Table 2.5 shows the eight possible combinations (with the median for each procedural

Table 2.5 Aggregate State Totals by Analysis Scores

Fiscal Analysis Score (Score Above 6)	Executive Review Score (Score Above 6)	Legislative Review (Score Above 5)	Average Number of Economic Rules (and no. of states with > median no. of economic rules)
Below	Below	Below	235 (2 of 3 above)
Below	Below	Above	212 (27 above)
Below	Above	Below	91 (0 of 2 above)
Below	Above	Above	167 (1 of 2 above)
Above	Below	Below	306 (2 of 3 above)
Above	Below	Above	197 (1 of 1 above)
Above	Above	Below	197 (2 of 5 above)
Above	Above	Above	108 (1 of 5 above)

score used to differentiate between states that use the procedure and states that do not).

The most striking result in this table is that the two highest average regulatory outputs occur in the states with scores for executive and legislative review that are below the median and two of the three lowest outputs occur where they are both above the median. The sample sizes are small, so appropriate caution should be taken here. That said, this pattern may indicate that a lack of political oversight from either political branch may lead to a greater output of regulations. No discernible pattern emerges regarding the use of economic analysis in combination with the other controls.

We also tested the relationship between rulemaking output and the combination of deadlines and other controls. It is possible that deadlines are more of a constraint when agencies have to complete analyses and go through executive or legislative review as part of the regulatory process. We found a statistically significant difference (at the 5 percent level using a one-sided t-test) between the mean number of economic rules in states with stringent executive review and deadlines, and states without stringent executive review or deadlines.[20] States with deadlines and executive review produced fewer economic rules (92) than states with deadlines and lax executive review (185). Legislative review and analysis showed differences in the same direction but did not rise to the level of statistical significance.

Politics and Procedures

Our final examination of this data involved combinations of the procedural control variables and political control of the branches of government.[21] First we looked at executive review in combination with the party of the sitting governor. The results are in Table 2.6.

Table 2.6 Gubernatorial Party Control and Executive Review

Party Control	Executive Review Score (Score Above 6)	Average No. of Economic + Licensing Regulations (and no. of states with > median no. of economic rules)
D	Below	209
		(5/10 above average)
D	Above	162
		(4/11 above average)
R	Below	304
		(2/4 above but 2 highest)
R	Above	89
		(0/3 above average)

The result in the last line is the most interesting one. While executive review by itself seems to show an impact on regulatory output only when it is at an extreme level (see discussion above), there does seem to be an important interaction with political control of the governor's office.

Specifically, in the three states where a Republican is governor and there is stringent executive review, a far smaller number of regulations with an economic impact are issued. This difference is statistically significant using a one-sided t-test, whether comparing these three states with the remaining twenty-five states (at the 1 percent level) or with the four states with Republican governors and no executive review (at the 10 percent level). It is possible that executive review makes little difference if there is a Democratic governor but that a Republican governor can use it to stifle regulation.

The situation looks similar, but with some important differences, when one examines the individual policy areas. Table 2.7 reproduces Table 2.6 by policy area. Each cell contains the average number of rules in that policy area.

As with the aggregate data, three of the five policy areas show the lowest volume of rulemaking when a Republican is governor and there is stringent executive review.[22] The opposite situation holds for agriculture, but there is only one state in this category for which we were able gather data on agricultural rulemaking. Interestingly, environmental rules, often seen as the most contentious area of regulation, show no relationship with this combination of gubernatorial variables.

We also examined legislative review in conjunction with party control of the legislature. The data is in Table 2.8.

Here the difference occurs on the other end of the spectrum. States in which Democrats control the legislature, and there is weak legislative review, tend to have a higher number of regulations. The difference between this group and the combination of the other three groups is significant using a one-sided t-test at the 5 percent level. Four of the five individual policy areas show the same pattern of highest rulemaking volume when Democrats control the legislature and legislative review is limited. The difference rises to statistical significance, however, only for insurance/banking.

Table 2.7 Gubernatorial Party Control and Executive Review by Policy Area

Party Control	Executive Review Score (Indicates Score Below/Above 6)	Environment	Agriculture	Insurance/ Banking	Education	Transportation
D	Below 6	30	13	16	26	7
D	Above 6	22	7	11	18	6
R	Below 6	27	13	18	34	21
R	Above 6	24	24	8	3	5

Table 2.8 Legislative Review and Legislative Control

Party Control (2007)	Legislative Review Score (Score Above 5)	Average No. of Economic + Licensing Regulations (and no. of states with > median no. of economic rules)
D	Below	355
		(4/4 above)
D	Above	161
		(3/7 above)
R	Below	167
		(2/8 above)
R	Above	169
		(2/9 above)

It appears that review by legislatures and executives may make a difference in regulatory output, but only if the existing coalition uses the review function. On the executive side this means that executive review makes it easier for a Republican governor to dull regulatory output. Executive review may be helpful but not sufficient to deter rulemaking. On the legislative side this means that regulatory output could be restrained either by strong legislative review or by having a legislature controlled by Republicans. Legislative review may be sufficient but not necessary to deter regulation.

2.4 DISCUSSION

Our primary finding about the effectiveness of procedures is that many of them have little impact on the volume of rulemaking unless accompanied by the political will to enforce them. Legislative review and economic impact analysis requirements appear to have little effect on the amount of regulation. Executive review may deter regulation, but this effect is most pronounced when a Republican controls the governor's mansion.

One procedure that has a clear effect on the pursuit of regulation is the requirement that agencies complete rulemaking within a prescribed time frame. Completion deadlines are a bit different than the other reforms discussed in this chapter. They have an absolute quality to them that removes discretion from the hands of existing coalitions. Either the agency finalizes the proposal by the deadline or they do not. By putting this type of deadline on agencies, enacting coalitions can reduce the volume of agency rulemaking. While legislatures and governors should be careful that any such deadlines are realistic, these deadlines may both control agency decision-making and lead to "good government" by not allowing agencies to linger over decisions for years.

While coalitions enacting procedural requirements appear to have limited influence over future agency decisions, all hope is not lost for those supporting political control of agency officials. Partisan control of the legislature had a clear effect on the volume of rulemaking. States with Democratic legislatures issued more regulations than states with Republican legislatures. We believe that this is likely due to the passage of laws requiring regulations by Democratic-controlled legislatures but lack the data to confirm this hypothesis.

The politics that matters the most are the politics of the moment. Existing coalitions, either through their passage of statutes, their use of long-recognized controls on agency behaviors such as the appointment power and budgetary control, or even their use of procedural controls put in place by prior coalitions, exhibit considerable impact on agency behavior. While we did not look at the substance of the 5000+ regulations tabulated, the relationship between existing coalitions and the level of regulations is highly suggestive that legislatures are critical in the decisions made by agencies.

The data in this chapter present a case that regulatory reform is not as effective as either its supporters or critics imagine. If regulatory reform does not give enacting coalitions power, then it is unlikely that it helps interest groups of any particular stripe (powerful interests, public-minded interests, or the expert community). To the extent that regulatory reforms confer power on a party, it appears, as Horn and Shepsle (1989) predicted, to be the existing coalitions that benefit. A sitting governor can use executive review to stifle regulation if (s)he is ideologically disposed to do so.

For those who have argued about the paralysis or ossification of the rulemaking process, our results are a mixed bag. Blind opposition to economic analysis or legislative review on the basis that such reforms would deter rulemaking finds no support from the data presented here. Executive review may discourage agencies from regulation, but supporters of regulation may better serve themselves by opposing governors opposed to regulations than by fighting over procedures. However, the fact that completion deadlines on rulemaking appear to deter regulation may give some support to those arguing that the rulemaking process is ossified. It is possible that the deadlines lead to fewer rules because it takes agencies time to navigate the procedural environment of rulemaking. As we will see in Chapter Three, deadlines may also discourage agencies from making changes in response to public comments. More procedures coupled with deadlines may mean fewer rules.

The 112th U.S. Congress debated numerous bills on regulatory reform. This debate was heavy on rhetoric about the evils or benefits of regulations and very light on the empirical impact of regulatory reform. Numerous studies of the federal rulemaking process have made valuable contributions to debates on regulatory reform, but questions about the efficacy of regulatory procedures remain, and the degree to which enacting and existing coalitions of politicians control agency decisions remains open. The results of this chapter suggest that the effects of regulatory reforms are limited unless there is the political will to implement them.

In the next chapter we examine a case study of the impacts of regulatory reform. While the aggregate data are suggestive, it is hard to draw firm conclusions without knowing more about the actual operation of regulatory reforms. What does the evidence in one state say about the effect of regulatory reform/procedural controls? Are there concrete examples of regulatory reforms making a difference in regulations? How do agency officials and outside interests perceive the role of regulatory procedures? We address these questions, using data from the state of New Jersey, in the next chapter.

3   In the Regulatory Weeds of the Garden State
A Case Study

> We must work harder to create a regulatory system that carries out the mandates of the law more effectively and at the same time reduces delay and minimizes burdens for our citizens; and . . . we must be willing to continually improve the regulatory system, to ensure that it promotes economic development in this State.
>
> New Jersey Governor
> August 2, 1993

> New Jersey must simultaneously move toward reducing redundant and unnecessary regulation that dulls the State's competitive advantage while being ever vigilant in the protection of the public's health, safety and welfare.
>
> New Jersey Governor
> November 2, 1994

Uttered just a year apart, these executive proclamations reflect the tone of the debate that has been taking place in the Garden State over the past three decades. In the first instance, the Governor was James Florio, a Democrat; the second public statement was issued by his Republican successor, Christine Todd Whitman. Despite their party differences, both chief executives focused on regulatory reforms while trumpeting a pervasive theme: Regulations are harmful when they impede economic growth and stymie businesses; at the same time, regulations are at their best when they safeguard the environment and protect public health. Striking this balance has often been elusive for policy-makers. New Jersey is home to a vibrant petrochemical and pharmaceutical industry, situated in the most densely populated state in the nation. The state is also recognized as having some of the most stringent environmental laws in the country, including the first-in-the-nation Worker and Community Right to Know Act and the New Jersey Freshwater Wetlands Act, both of which exceeded federal standards when enacted. Today, the political rhetoric that pervades the regulatory reform debate has changed little, just as the public's demands and expectations from policy-makers remain the same.

While the state's governors have used executive orders and State of the State addresses to tout their regulatory reforms and overhaul plans, New Jersey legislators have not been content to be bystanders. Legislators have attempted to shape the regulatory climate by passing more than half a dozen major regulatory reform initiatives over the last few decades. These measures included procedures requiring agencies to conduct numerous analyses of their regulations in the name of greater accountability and transparency. Negotiated rulemaking can now be triggered in certain circumstances, and public participation forums are often mandated, and have increased in number. All of this comes on top of the notice and comment process that is common to rulemaking in most states, and at the federal level. The most prominent of these reforms was a constitutional referendum, approved by the voters, which empowers the legislature with veto power over any and all regulations.

Despite these continual changes to the regulatory process, the drumbeat for further change among the stakeholders remains a constant theme. From business leaders to environmental advocates, there is a perception that agencies continue to overreach their authority when it comes to implementing laws. This fact alone gives support to the argument that previous regulatory reforms have failed to achieve their stated goals. Two regulatory transactions in particular reflect this common frustration.

In the first instance, it was the business sector that felt betrayed by the regulatory process. After twenty months of public hearings, legislative committee debates, and scores of amendments embedded in a 200-plus page proposal, a law was enacted that gave workers and community residents access to information about hazardous chemicals used and stored in the workplace.[1] At the heart of the controversy was a labeling provision that required disclosure of health and safety information regarding those substances being used in the manufacturing processes or stored on-site at facilities. From the outset, the provision was drafted to protect trade secrets while providing health and emergency response personnel with essential information if exposure resulted from a chemical release or a spill. Still, a significant question remained unanswered.

Was it possible to label the hazardous substances that pass through miles of pipelines inside a petroleum or chemical manufacturing plant? Complicating the practicality of the labeling requirement was an acknowledgment by all parties that manufacturing processes often change within a work cycle, if not by the hour. A compromise was ultimately struck between the bill's sponsor and the regulated community: The labeling of hazardous substances would only be required at the valves which ultimately control the flow of chemicals into the pipelines. Despite *explicit* statutory language stipulating this provision, the initial regulations proposed by the Department of Environmental Protection (DEP) contained language that mandated a more comprehensive labeling requirement that went well beyond the stipulated and publicly articulated legislative compromise. The proposed regulatory language was only withdrawn after the sponsor personally expressed his objections to the DEP Commissioner. In an interview, the former Senator recalled that the environmental community had attempted to make gains with environmental regulators that were not secured during the legislative process. Although he felt the legislative intent was clear, he observed that he also held a unique form of leverage in the regulatory process as he chaired the Senate Energy and Environment Committee, which oversaw the regulatory agency charged with implementing the rules.

More than a decade later, environmental advocates felt similarly disadvantaged by the regulatory proceedings. In 1999 the state passed a comprehensive energy deregulation law that was designed to lower the state's high utility rates and, in the process, spur competition among energy suppliers, including those marketers who offered cleaner and pollution-free products.[2] In this case, most of the implementation details were deferred to the regulatory agency, the Board of Public Utilities (BPU).[3]

Under the law, utility companies were directed to offer default service—to become, in effect, the provider of last resort. This provision was intended to spur competition by encouraging energy suppliers to enter a competitive market where more than three million residential customers were up for grabs.[4] This competitive marketplace was welcomed by environmental organizations who believed providers of clean and renewable energy products would be attracted to a state market where they could compete on both price and value-added content.

While competition was robust at the outset, with more than two dozen companies competing for gas and electric customers, the BPU proposed another set of regulations just as the temporary rate caps were expiring in order to transition to market-based pricing.[5] These regulations represented a stark deviation from the statute, according to one marketer interviewed. And in this case, there were no legislative sponsors, no legislative oversight chairs, and no one who currently held power objecting to the changed approach—which was occurring years after the initial passage of the Act.

The key provision dealt with the so-called "default service"—a provision originally designed to allow market retailers the opportunity to compete for customers who did not "switch away" from the incumbent utility. The regulatory change proposed by the BPU transformed the market by establishing a wholesale auction. Under this scenario, the utilities were directed to aggregate their load and solicit bids at a wholesale price that they in turn would pass directly on to those customers that did not "switch away." In addition to allowing the utilities to keep all of its customers in a deregulated market, the regulatory provision set up a marketplace in which the *retailers* were now competing for customers who were being offered an aggregated *wholesale* commodity. Fundamentally, the wholesale commodity did not include marketing and acquisition expenses borne by the retail marketers for whom the market was established.

The price differential advantaged the utility by more than 20 percent (two to five cents per kWh). The regulatory impact was measurable—less than

2 percent of electric customers switched away from their utility provider, the so-called "provider of last resort."[6] Today, most of the clean energy suppliers that were operating in the market before the rules were finalized have left the state due to the imposition of the artificial rates set exclusively through BPU rules,[7] despite numerous regulatory reforms that were passed with the hope of improving agency fealty to legislative intent.

These narratives are not isolated stories, but they help illustrate both the frequent calls for regulatory reform among the stakeholders and the fruitlessness of the reforms that have been implemented.

3.1   A HISTORICAL OVERVIEW OF REGULATORY REFORM IN NEW JERSEY

Of the half dozen statutory reforms enacted since the passage of the state Administrative Procedure Act—from impact analyses,[8] broader public hearing and comment requirements to the initiation of a regulation by petition[9]—the lion's share of the procedural reforms have been added over the last thirty years. During the same period, almost every sitting governor had his or her own version of an executive order[10] directing comprehensive reviews of the state's regulatory system, with very few tangible changes taking place. At work today in the State Capitol, Governor Chris Christie has issued four Executive Orders targeted at decreasing the number of regulations on the books.

Historically, the legislative modifications that have occurred cannot be traced to partisan leadership. While four of the initiatives were signed into law by Republican governors, half the measures were advanced during sessions led by legislative leaders of the opposition party. The reforms also evolved through fits and starts rather than through broad mandates or public support. Today, New Jersey has more requirements for "impact statements" than any other state in the nation.

The changes made in the 1980s and 1990s were, according to the rhetoric that accompanied their passage, attempts to minimize the effect of regulations on small businesses, farmers, levels of employment, and the general economy. Legislative leaders later added a Jobs Impact Statement (which quantifies the number of jobs lost or created by a proposed regulation) on top of existing requirements.[11] Moreover, for regulations impacting businesses with fewer than 100 employees, the legislature required a Regulatory Flexibility Analysis that describes any methods utilized to minimize the adverse economic impact on small businesses; from record-keeping, reporting, or compliance requirements. Another provision called for a Federal Standards Statement that requires an agency to address whether a proposed regulation exceeds federal standards. In the case when a federal standard will be exceeded, the agency must include a cost-benefit analysis supporting its decision while asserting that the proposed state standard is achievable under the current technology.

At the same time that these analysis requirements were being put in place by the legislature, executive attempts to enhance oversight of regulatory agencies were also taking place. This precipitated a turf battle from 1981 through 1992 over which branch would dominate the rulemaking process in the Garden State.

The first showdown occurred when a 1981 bipartisan measure allowing the legislature to approve and disapprove all regulatory proposals was vetoed by then Governor Thomas Kean, only to be overridden by the legislature. By the summer of the following year the state Supreme Court struck down the New Jersey Legislative Oversight Act as unconstitutional because it violated the separation of powers under the New Jersey Constitution.[12] The legislature did not retreat on its attempts to gain regulatory oversight authority. Ultimately, a second ballot initiative granting legislative veto authority was again presented to the voters for approval in 1992. This time the measure passed by a wide margin. Despite the decade-long bipartisan effort by legislative leaders to secure legislative veto authority, this power has rarely been fully exercised since the constitutional amendment became effective on December 3, 1992.

The regulatory process in New Jersey was again reformed in 2001. At the time, the legislation was described in press releases as a major overhaul of the Administrative Procedure Act (APA). Among the key components were increased transparency, including the publication of all agency fees, penalties, deadlines, and processing times, as well as a more widely disseminated public notice requirement and a required quarterly rulemaking calendar.[13] The changes also broadened public hearing requirements and allowed extensions to the comment period when sufficient public interest warrants. The law enhanced the petition process by setting strict deadlines for agencies to respond to petitions, limiting their discretion in the manner they responded and providing intervention by the Office of Administrative Law in the event an agency failed to comply.[14] Finally, a "standard of clarity" was applied to all regulatory activity, as was a requirement for a verbatim record of public hearings.

Since the 2001 law was enacted, a few new regulatory reforms have been adopted. Although we conducted our review in line with the version of the APA in effect during the study years, it is important to call attention to a new law enacted in March 2011, which allows an agency to avoid starting the regulatory process over from scratch if it wishes to significantly "enlarge or curtail who or what will be affected by the proposed regulation (P.L.2011, c.33)." In effect, an agency can now trigger an expedited sixty-day public comment period to examine the substantive change, after which it may issue a notice of adoption. We discuss the potential effect of this change later in this chapter.

An Ideal Setting

Given its history, New Jersey presents an interesting case study in which to explore the impact procedural reforms may have on the regulatory process.

No other state has adopted as many noneconomic impact requirements as New Jersey; six in total. Its constitution also provides for a strong chief executive and its legislature is considered a hybrid in terms of professionalism; yet its full-year calendar schedule and large staff resources make its characterization closer to that of the more professional legislatures.[15] The state's APA also mandates a fiscal analysis for all regulations, although the analysis is not conducted by an independent agency, nor is it a "cost-benefit" analysis. As noted earlier, it is one of only sixteen states that have legislative veto powers over regulations that do not require the approval of the governor.[16] Finally, the governor and legislative chambers have been controlled by both parties, which make it ideal for examining the influence of political ideologies.

All these factors make New Jersey an excellent state in which to investigate the influence of regulatory reforms. More specifically, we can ask: What role do rulemaking procedures play in the regulatory decision-making process? Procedures that encourage participation should lead to more participation and perhaps more acceptance of the suggestions made by participants. Procedures that require analysis should lead to analyses being conducted and regulations that are less costly. Procedures for legislative or executive review should lead to regulations that reflect the preferences of these political branches and occasional vetoes of the regulations that don't. These are the types of effects that we were not able to observe in the broader study in Chapter Two. We can also examine the question at the core of the previous chapter: If regulatory reforms deter agencies from engaging in regulatory activity, should we expect to find fewer regulations adopted as the level of procedural controls increases?

The analysis here is best read as a case study of the history and effects of regulatory reform in a single state. New Jersey is an excellent case study because of the sheer volume of regulatory reforms over the past few decades. As with all successful case studies, we are not explicitly testing hypotheses but raising questions about a commonly held perception, that regulatory reforms make a significant difference in regulatory output, and adding context to our broader conclusions in Chapter Two, which refute this perception.

As we will describe, we collected a large set of data on regulation in New Jersey and interviewed several knowledgeable participants in the New Jersey regulatory process. Together, this information largely supports the conclusions of the previous chapter that cast doubt on the idea that regulatory reforms play a major role in regulatory decision-making.

3.2 OUR DATA

In order to provide a contextual view of regulatory activity over the past decade, we collected data on the number of regulations issued from 1998 through 2007. We also examined in greater detail 1707 regulations in New

Jersey from two periods: 1998–1999 and 2006–2007. We gathered data on a number of variables capturing the administrative process in New Jersey. These included the number of comments received from the public, the length of the regulation, and the presence or absence of public hearings, agency response to comments, and re-proposals triggered by substantive changes. We also did a more detailed examination of the impact analyses of the most controversial regulations[17] issued in these four years.

We also collected individual units of datum[18] on a number of variables for the years 1997–1998 and 2006–2007. The variables measured included the type of regulations,[19] the promulgating agency,[20] whether the agency published the full text,[21] the page length of the regulation,[22] public comment entered into the record,[23] the total number of individuals who submitted written comments or signed a petition (if individually recorded by the agency), whether the agency held a public hearing as part of the public comment period, and, if a hearing was held, the number of individuals who attended.[24] Finally, we calculated the total public participation[25] and recorded the agency response.[26] As noted, we conducted a more detailed examination of the impact analyses of the most controversial regulations issued in these four years.

The four years for which we gathered longitudinal data represented a two-year period during a Republican-led administration (Christine Todd Whitman), and a two-year period during a Democratic-led administration (Jon Corzine). For each of the cycles, the legislative leaders in both chambers shared the same party affiliation as the governor. The years studied occurred closely *before* and *after* the enactment of what policy-makers described as procedural reforms adopted in 2001. Selecting this period would help measure the effect, if any, resulting from those changes to the regulatory process in New Jersey.

We selected the variables described above in order to capture the types of regulations that were issued in New Jersey in the years in question, the amount of participation, the complexity of the regulations (page length is our proxy for complexity), and how state agencies responded to procedures. To assess the role of other procedures such as impact analyses, we did a more detailed examination of those regulations with the most comments, expecting that regulations with the greatest impacts would lead to the most comments and that therefore we would expect the largest role of impact analysis to occur in these regulations.

In our analysis, we included only those regulations that resulted in a change in policy, as noted above. This means that we excluded readopted amendments, which do not alter existing regulations. Although New Jersey has a regulatory procedure that stipulates all rules must sunset after five years, for the most part, only 2 percent of sunsetted rules are readopted with substantive amendments (see Table 3.5). Agencies also do not publish the full text of these regulations in the notice of proposal or adoption in the New Jersey Register. By taking this approach, we exclusively looked at permanent changes made to existing requirements and new regulations.[27] We also excluded notices of administrative change/correction and temporary amendments as well as other non-regulatory public notices.

Finally, to improve the depth of our understanding of New Jersey regulatory activity and the role of procedures, we conducted interviews with six frequent participants in the regulatory process. These included individuals with experience in agencies as well as in outside groups with an interest in regulatory issues (some of the individuals had experience with regulatory activity both inside and outside of government). After asking the interview subjects about the history of their involvement with the regulatory process, we asked about the reforms we were interested in (notice and comment, analysis, legislative review, and regulatory negotiation) to get their experiences and perceptions of each one.

3.3 REFORM ON PAPER, NOT IN PRACTICE

The historical overview of the last ten years (1998–2007) reveals that the volume of regulatory activity has remained relatively unchanged in New Jersey. On average, annual regulatory activity over the period is 1350 regulations/year (Table 3.1). It is difficult to distinguish any party preference for regulations based upon the summary data. The average number of regulations proposed and adopted under a Republican administration (1998–2001) closely tracks that of two Democratic administrations (2002–2007).[28] Although regulations appear to have spiked in 1998, the results that year were due to a high proportion of new regulations that were triggered by expired regulations and one-time processes such as traffic control signalizations and drug formulary additions and deletions. A more detailed comparative analysis of the more substantive regulations adopted is displayed in Table 3.2.

Given our interest in exploring, or at least controlling for, differences in political ideologies, we chose to study 1998–1999 and 2006–2007. As noted, the earlier period represents two years when New Jersey was under Republican leadership and the later period reflects regulatory activity under Democratic leadership. We then culled the dataset (as described above) to include only those final regulations that made substantive changes to public policy (Table 3.2).

We caution the reader against interpreting the aggregate numbers as reflecting higher regulatory activity under the Republican leadership of the Whitman Administration. The fact that there were a greater number of regulations in 1998 can be largely attributed to two departments that had increased regulatory activity, namely the Department of Transportation (DOT) and the Department of Health and Senior Services (DHSS). The spike in 1998 is largely due to the number of adopted amendments for these two departments: DOT (60) and DHHS (40). Many of the DOT regulations dealt with traffic signalizations and many of the DHHS regulations covered

Table 3.1 All Calendar Year Regulatory Activity (1998–2007)

Year	All Regulatory Activity[1]	Regulations Adopted	Regulations Proposed
1998	1502	640	613
1999	1259	508	521
2000	1223	572	478
2001	1396	543	529
2002	1290	466	490
2003	1430	587	551
2004	1432	593	528
2005	1397	549	537
2006	1345	563	475
2007	1230	480	431
10 Yr. Avg.	1350	550	529

[1] Beginning with the March 7, 2005 issue, two regulatory activities became electronically available via the NJ Register: the "Register Index of Regulation Proposals and Adoptions" and the "Rulemaking in this Issue" notice. These additions slightly overstate the annual amount of regulatory activity, including notices of proposals and adoptions. As such, the totals for both these types of notices were removed from the counts for 2005, 2006, and 2007.

drug formularies. These types of regulations, traffic operations and drug utilization reviews, were not found in any significant number in the 2006 and 2007 years, further explaining the atypical volume in 1998.

Once this anomaly is corrected, we see a slight decrease in regulation between 1998–1999 and 2006–2007. We then examined which agencies did the most regulating during these years. The cabinet-level agencies were among the most prolific regulators. Of the twenty-two agencies examined, which included independent authorities and commissions, ten agencies accounted for more than three-quarters (81.1 percent) of all regulations adopted on average over the four-year study period. The same ten agencies were the most prolific rule makers in both study periods. This consistency

Table 3.2 Substantive Regulations Adopted (1998–1999 and 2006–2007)

Year	Number of Regulations
1998	550
1999	405
2006	399
2007	353
Total	1707

Table 3.3 Percentage of Regulations Adopted by Department

Top 10 Ranked Agencies	1998–99	2006–2007
Health & Senior Services (DHSS)	13.2%	8.0%
Law & Public Safety (DLPS)	11.3%	16.2%
Transportation (DOT)	10.9%	3.7%
Human Services (DHS)	10.4%	8.0%
Casino Control Commission (CCC)	7.9%	5.2%
Treasury (TRES)	6.8%	10.5%
Environmental Protection (DEP)	6.1%	7.2%
Banking & Insurance (B&I)	6.1%	8.6%
Community Affairs (DCA)	5.9%	10.1%
Labor (DOL)	4.2%	4.9%

reveals a lack of distinction between Republican and Democratic adminis-trations. Where we do see large shifts between the periods, can be explained by departmental realignments, as in the case of the Treasury, which now houses former divisions from the Department of State in 2006–2007, and one-time rulemaking surges such as the traffic signalization rulemakings at DOT in 1998, as presented in Table 3.3.

3.4 THE ROLE OF PUBLIC PARTICIPATION

If the overall volume of regulation and the agencies promulgating regu-lations did not change much during different gubernatorial tenures, how about the substantive effects of the various regulatory reforms? At the very center of all regulatory activity is the public participation process. The vol-ume of input (as measured by number of comments) *and* output of public participation (as measured by agency changes due to comment) suggests only a modest impact. To begin, the public commented on half (51 percent) of the 1707 regulations adopted during the study period. Forty-nine percent of adopted regulations were commented on by the public in 1998, 50 per-cent in 1999, and 52 percent in both 2006 and 2007.

A total of 17,409 written comments were aimed at 868 of the total 1707 regulations during the study years. The number of comments for any given regulation ranged from one to 1624, but about half of the regulations that received comments (53 percent) received two comments or fewer. The mean number of comments received per regulation was 20.06; however, this average is misleading due to a skewed distribution (the median is 2.25). Thirty regulations received over 100 comments, which amounted to 68 percent (11,809) of the total comments submitted. If you adjust for this skew (by eliminating those thirty regulations that received 100 or more comments), the average number of comments received was just slightly more than three comments per regulation (3.34); the median was zero. This difference between the mean and median also occurs at the federal level, and reflects the tendency of a few regulations to generate most of the comments from the public (Shapiro 2007).

Another regulatory reform intended to increase access to the regulatory process is the public hearing requirement. For the 1707 regulations adopted, 275 public hearings were held during the study period; however, the overall number of hearings held on regulations adopted steadily declined over the period, from ninety-five hearings in 1998, seventy-four in 1999, sixty in 2006, and forty-six in 2007. A total of 633 individuals attended the public hearings, although participation did not always mean an attendee offered comments into the record. While it appears, on average, as if two members of the public participated in each hearing, in actuality, only about a quarter of all public hearings (28 percent) were attended by members of the public. Attendance by the public numbered as few as one person to a high of forty-two people; the mean was 8.12 attendees, the median attendance was three, and the mode was one attendee for the seventy-eight hearings in which the public participated.

On its face, the amount of public participation that was generated, both oral and written, was limited over the entire study period. Still, we were left to wonder if participation increased after the regulatory reforms broadening public access to the regulatory process went into effect in July 2001. Recall, the key components included a more widely disseminated public notice requirement, agency compliance with a regular quarterly rulemaking calendar, extended public comment periods, and a public hearing requirement when and if sufficient public interest warranted, as well as the maintenance of a verbatim record of the public hearing.

In total, the number of regulations that received comments was nearly identical in the four years. It even appears that participation, as measured by the number of comments received, both written and oral, actually declined slightly between 1998 (5228) and 2007 (4762), as displayed in Table 3.4. However, when this number is divided by the number of regulations adopted, participation/regulation actually increased from 9.51 participants per regulation in 1998 to 13.49 participants per regulation in 2007 (Table 3.4). No change in format submission has occurred to explain the percentage increase; all comments must still be submitted to the regulating agency in writing rather than electronically. What has changed is the publication and distribution of the regulatory calendar.

The 2001 reforms may be responsible for this increase in the number of comments per regulation submitted. It is also possible that the increased proliferation of email between the study periods provided interest groups with more resources to organize their membership and get them to send comments on particularly salient regulations. While the mean number of comments has increased, the median remains one for all study years, as shown in

Table 3.4 Level of Public Comment Participation (1998–1999 and 2006–2007)

Level of Participation	Total	1998	1999	2006	2007
Total Regulation (n)	1707	550	405	399	353
Regulations Receiving Comments (n)	893	288	211	208	186
Total Participation (n)	18,042	5228	3067	4985	4762
Mean Comments/ Regulation	10.57	9.52	7.57	12.49	13.49
Median	1	1	1	1	1
Minimum	0	0	0	0	0
Maximum	1624	1152	417	1624	1103

Table 3.4. This reveals that the increased participation per regulation is due to a small number of regulations, so it is more likely that a few more controversial regulations caused the aggregate increase in public participation. Because our ability to examine the affiliation of the commenters is limited, we cannot determine the extent to which the increase in comments is due to increased interest group mobilization.

When a longtime Statehouse insider who represents a trade association and regularly appears in front of regulators to submit comments or give oral testimony was asked if agencies make changes in response to public comments, he replied, "Typically no." He added, ". . . but depending on the magnitude of the issue and the potential negative impact from a monetary standpoint, agencies may make changes to regulations."

3.5 INFLUENCE OF TIME CONSTRAINTS

We also assessed the end of the regulatory process to determine the impact public participation had on regulations. As noted earlier, all regulations have to be adopted within a year of the proposal publication; if not, the proposed regulation expires. As discussed in Chapter Two, deadlines are the one procedural control that appears to dampen rulemaking output. Additionally, if substantive changes were proposed during the years we studied, the regulation needed to be re-proposed—this resets the time clock. Starting over clearly lengthens the regulatory process, which may have made agencies more resistant to adopt substantive changes offered during the public participation process.

We took a look at the number of notices of re-proposals for the entire ten-year period (see Table 3.5).[29]

We found less than 2 percent of all final regulations were substantively changed enough to trigger the re-proposal requirement. The mean for the ten-year period was 8.3 regulations and the median was eight, with a range

Table 3.5 Reproposed Amendments Triggered by Substantive Changes

	1998	1999	2000	2001	2002	2003	2004	2005	2006	2007
Re-proposed Amendments	9	16	9	8	10	7	8	5	5	6

of five to sixteen. Once again the data indicates a limited impact for public comments. One agency official explained this to us:

> We consult with stakeholders as we draft regulations and many changes are made in draft regulations before we formally propose a regulation amendment. Therefore we don't often need to make substantive changes once a regulation has been officially proposed.

This supports the observation by West (2009) that many regulatory decisions are set before a proposed regulation is even issued.[30]

3.6 AGENCIES CONTROL THE GAME

Aside from the substantive change trigger, a regulatory proposal may be amended prior to adoption if the changes do not ". . . effectively enlarge or curtail the original proposal, change its effect or those who will be affected . . ."[31] Both kinds of changes, substantive and technical, must be recorded by an agency as part of the adoption notice; changes may take the form of a "Summary of Agency Initiated Changes," a "Summary of Changes Upon Adoption," and/or a "Response to a Comment." Of the total regulations examined (1707), only 477 regulations (28 percent) were modified by the agency after the regulation was proposed. By comparison, there was also a slight decrease in the percentage of agency changes made in the latter study years, despite the 2001 regulatory reform that broadened public participation. Overall, 29 percent of the final regulations adopted were changed in 1998 and 30 percent in 1999, as compared to 25 percent in 2006 and 27 percent in 2007. We have no hypotheses explaining this decrease, but it is interesting that even after the changes to broaden participation in 2001, agencies infrequently changed regulations in response to participation

In some ways, one stakeholder we interviewed believed the deck is stacked in favor of the agencies. An attorney who has been involved with regulatory policy for thirty-five years observed that while he has seen small changes frequently made by agencies in response to comments, he "rarely [sees] major changes that significantly divert from the agency's original proposal." Given the low level of responsiveness, we then asked what course of action he pursues or recommends to clients when a regulation turns out contrary to his interests. He described the limited options in this way: "I have never gone to the Appellate Division [since] the defer-to-agency-expertise hurdle is too high. I have gone to the Legislature. . . . I have also asked for a sponsor's help during a rulemaking" by asking for a letter to be sent to the agency during the comment period.[32]

Given the small percentage of changes made following the public participation period, we did a more detailed examination of the agency responses to comments in the most controversial regulations issued in these four years. Over the four-year study period, agencies received 100 or more comments on just thirty regulations; there were only three regulations for which agencies seemed to make meaningful changes.[33]

Finally, a number of our interview subjects specifically voiced frustration with agency responsiveness. Ironically, this perspective was also shared by a former senior DEP manager who was heavily involved in his agency's regulatory activities. "While the agency generally wanted to be responsive to public comments, there was a strong incentive to adopt regulations without substantive changes as republication of the revised regulation was required under the APA," said one of our interview subjects. Another stakeholder said, "In my history, I remember few if any actual changes of substance made in response to comments." The requirement to re-propose clearly acts as a disincentive for agencies to make changes in response to public comments. One respondent also suggested modifying the APA to allow agencies to make changes without wholesale re-proposal.

> One of the key problems with the public comment process arises from the difficulty agencies face in making substantive changes to published regulation proposals based on public comment. The fact that agencies generally have to repropose as if they were starting from scratch provides a huge disincentive to fix problems with regulations as published. This argues for a modified and shorter process for substantive changes . . . after public comment, and careful discussion with stakeholders prior to publication of regulations. . . .

This last comment was gathered during an October 2010 interview; since that time, the APA was amended to do exactly what the interview subject suggested. In a law enacted in March of 2011, agencies may now separate substantive changes from their initial regulation proposal in order to hold a shorter and more comprehensive review of the particular provision being substantially changed. It will be important to return to New Jersey in the future to see if this change has allowed agencies to be more responsive to public comments. Additionally, case studies in states where regulatory activities are limited[34] would be a good place to examine if a relationship exists between regulatory deadlines and an agency's responsiveness to public comments. Of particular interest would be an investigation of whether there is a correlation between time limits and the likelihood an agency will make changes to a proposal that receives public input, if amending the proposal serves to lengthen the adoption process.

3.7 IMPACT ANALYSES: GOOD, BAD, OR NO DIFFERENCE

Debates over the role of impact analysis in regulatory activity have occurred at the federal level for some time now. It is not surprising to find both economic and other impact analyses have been adopted as part of reform initiatives advanced in the states. In New Jersey, agencies have been required to conduct some form of impact analyses on their regulations since 1981. Our analysis of agency regulations changes triggered by these impact analyses focused on those regulations with at least 100 comments. We believed that those regulations with the most comments were likely to be the ones with the largest economic impacts. In addition to triggering an economic analysis, these regulations may have also triggered analyses examining an agency's regulatory flexibility, the regulations' impacts on jobs, or whether federal standards are exceeded.

Of the thirty regulations with more than 100 comments, only four had impact statements that contained actual numbers to describe the economic impact of the regulation. Two of the regulations were issued by the Department of Environmental Protection. One on protecting Highlands water[35] had a detailed analysis of the economic impact. A second regulation protecting horseshoe crabs[36] had information on fish catches and the tourism industry but did not have a conclusion about the economic impact. A third regulation on a surcharge on goods sold in prisons described the total revenue that the agency expected to generate (not an economic impact per se).[37] Finally, a regulation on Medicaid reimbursements for nursing homes similarly totaled the expected budgetary effects without a meaningful assessment of economic impacts.[38]

The remaining regulations either had a brief qualitative discussion of economic impacts or simply asserted that there would be no impact. An example of a qualitative discussion could be found in a regulation prohibiting certain trucks from certain state roads.[39]

> Double-trailer truck combinations and 102-inch wide standard trucks not doing business in New Jersey will be prohibited from using state highways and county roads as through routes or short cuts. This may have a negative impact on those truckers and shippers since it may take longer to arrive at their destinations, thus making it more costly, or it could cost more in tolls compared to some parallel routes.

With such cursory attention given to economic impacts, it is hard to argue that the requirement for any of the impact analyses has had much of an effect in New Jersey.[40]

This impression was reinforced by the interview subjects, who uniformly minimized the role of analyses, with one saying, "I would have to say that the required analyses played a relatively small role." Another director of an NGO who regularly participates in regulatory proceedings said that he "rarely" paid any attention to the mandated impact analyses since they are ". . . generally not about the key policy issues and have the appearance of being rather canned." Instead the pattern seems to be an even starker example of what some scholars have said occurs at the federal level. Impact analyses seem to be written after the regulation to justify the regulation rather than used to influence the regulatory decision being made (Hahn et al. 2000).

3.8 ADDITIONAL REFORMS

We also looked at parts of the regulatory process outside of the standard notice and comment procedure. Utilization of the procedural tool known as the "notice of preproposal" allowing agencies to "test the waters" before engaging in regulatory proceedings on complex and controversial matters has also failed to gain traction with policy-makers of either party. Of the fifty-four preproposals filed over the ten-year period, only the Department of Education made use of the process with any consistency for a total of sixteen notices, led primarily by its policy-making arm, the State Board of Education. Notices of preproposal ranged from a low of one in 1999 to a high of twelve in 2002 (see Table 3.6).

An additional process available to agencies interested in gathering feedback on a contemplated regulation is to request the Office of Administrative Law (OAL) conduct a preliminary, non-adversarial proceeding on the proposal. However, agencies have not utilized this process, referred to as "negotiating a regulation," according to one OAL administrator that we spoke with who was familiar with the regulatory procedures in the state since 1986.

Another procedural change, made in 2001, was the requirement establishing stricter deadlines for agencies to respond to requests for regulations initiated by public petition—those regulatory proposals initiated by other than agency bureaucrats. In addition to setting deadlines for the agency to respond to a petition, the agency is now directed as to its response: It must grant the petition, deny the petition, or refer the petition for further deliberation. Despite these procedural modifications to the petition mechanism, it does not appear that regulations initiated by the public were advanced by the agency at a higher rate.

We also found that agencies do have regulatory seasons, which may produce a spike in activity in any given calendar year. The most frequent triggers to regulatory activity include new legislation and regulations expiring due to sunset provisions. We did not find increased activity in the first years of a gubernatorial term when we review the volume of rulemaking from 1998 through 2007; however, we did find increased regulatory activity during the final year of a sitting governor's term (2001, 2005). This transition in power may represent another reason for an annual increase in regulatory activity (O'Connell 2008).

Our comparison of the study years leaves open the question as to whether there is an increase in the complexity of the regulations adopted. The

Table 3.6 Notice of Prepoposals in Advance of Proposals

Rule Activity	1998	1999	2000	2001	2002	2003	2004	2005	2006	2007
Regulation Proposal	613	521	478	529	490	551	528	575	523	479
Notice of Pre-Proposal	6	1	4	9	12	4	6	7	3	2

average page length per regulation increased from 11.97 in 1998 and 14.33 in 1999 to 17.2 in 2006 and 16.8 in 2007. Page length generally correlates both with complexity of a regulation and with the number of comments an agency receives, particularly due to the APA requirement that each distinct comment must be responded to by the agency. Therefore, more comments may also be the reason for longer regulatory documents. We are unable to differentiate between these two possible causes for increased page length (complexity and number of comments).

3.9 THE LEGISLATIVE VETO

The procedural change with the potential to have the greatest impact on regulations for all years emanates from the state's constitutional provision that grants legislative oversight. Although the legislature has had veto authority over regulations for the past twenty-one years, it has rarely exercised the power. On occasion, members of the legislature have sponsored concurrent resolutions, but the number introduced has averaged around thirteen per session over the last twelve years leading up to the period of our study. During that time frame, three concurrent resolutions were passed by both chambers, which served thirty day notice on the agency to amend or withdraw the existing or proposed regulation or regulation. In each case, a second concurrent resolution invalidating or prohibiting the regulation or regulation did not follow.

The absence of use of a legislative veto may signal that there is a more informal means to the same end. When asked to describe the involvement of the New Jersey legislature in his agency's regulatory process, one former senior official characterized it in this way:

> Occasionally, a proposed regulation would be controversial enough that an individual legislator of even a committee would express concerns, and hold a hearing. There were also several oversight committees which sometimes held hearings on DEP proposed regulations at the request of the regulated community. While there were indeed some rare policy differences that motivated some of this legislative oversight, more often than not it was simply a case where the legislator was taking the agency to task for political gain, and it appeared that we were doing exactly what the legislation directed us to do.

Here the threat of a veto (having the power) may be as powerful as an actual veto given the practice that a legislature, or an individual member, has other ex-ante mechanisms available to get an agency's attention. In Chapter Seven, we conduct in-depth interviews with policy-makers and stakeholders in two states, North Carolina and Pennsylvania, where there are strong legislative or independent review powers. In Pennsylvania, we are able to more closely examine how the Independent Regulatory Review Commission (IRRC) is used as an ex-ante mechanism by the legislature to deliver service to constituents.

The lack of an actual veto ever being exercised in New Jersey may also be linked to the notion that legislatures are less willing to veto a regulation when the two branches of government are headed by members of the same political party. As an example, when Governor Corzine left office, he had signed into law a measure that allows the sale and use of medical marijuana by prescription. The implementation of this law was left to the incoming governor, Chris Christie, who is on record as opposing the law. Today, medical marijuana is still not available by prescription as the proposed regulations were at first delayed and then drafted in a way that eviscerated the original intent of the law, according to proponents of the measure. At one point, the Democrats in the legislature introduced a concurrent regulation to veto the rules. In response, the Department of Health and Senior Services withdrew the provisions in the rule that conflicted directly with statutory language and proposed a new rule for consideration.

Historically, since the constitutional change occurred in late 1992, New Jersey's government has been split along partisan lines for just four years during those two decades. Notably, the legislature placed the constitutional amendment on the ballot following eight years of split governance in which the governor was a Republican and the Senate was under Democratic control. This observation is supported by the research of other scholars (Huber, Shipan, and Pfahler 2001; Daley et al. 2007) who argue that unified legislatures have greater controls over bureaucracy while legislatures in divided governments are viewed as more influential when they possess absolute veto powers over regulations.

3.10 LOOKING AHEAD

In New Jersey we found that agencies are largely immune to the regulatory reforms implemented by governors and legislatures. This case study supports our findings in Chapter Two. Substantive changes to agency proposals as a result of comments are rare. They may be made even rarer by another procedure, the requirement that substantial changes to a proposed regulation necessitate a re-proposal. Impact analyses are pro forma at best. The legislative veto power has not been exercised by the New Jersey state legislature to invalidate an executive branch regulation since at least 1996.[41] Negotiated rulemaking has also never been utilized over the past twenty years by an agency. At the end of the day, the volume of regulatory activity is largely unchanged over the past decade despite changes in administration, and the addition of procedural requirements.

While the debate over the proceduralization of the regulatory process at the federal level has been inconclusive, this examination of the administrative process in New Jersey supports the argument that many of these regulatory reforms are epiphenomenal. In effect, they have little impact on the substance of the regulations they are designed to affect. They also do little to discourage regulation or overly burden agencies.

Even notice and comment, the oldest of regulatory procedures, appears to play a limited role in New Jersey regulatory decision-making. Fewer than 2 percent of all regulations are re-proposed in New Jersey, indicating that significant changes to agency proposals are rare. Of the remaining regulations, very few have anything but the most minor changes. This is true even in those regulations receiving more than 100 comments.

For the more recent brand of regulatory reforms, the lack of impact is even starker. Requirements for various types of analysis also appear to have no effect. Of the analyses examined in this dataset, very few had actual numbers and even fewer (one by the estimation of these authors) measured true economic impact. The impact of economic analysis requirements appears to be even more limited than similar requirements at the federal level. In fact, the impact analyses appear to be little more than superficial window dressing in the regulatory preamble.

Other regulatory procedures are similarly limited. Legislative review has resulted in only three regulations being challenged over the last twelve years. Petitions for regulations are routinely dismissed by agencies (although less frequently since 2001). The one change that may have had an impact is the 2001 effort to increase participation. But even this change had large effects only on the most controversial regulations and may be due to more effective interest group mobilization rather than the change in regulatory procedures.

Our twenty-eight state analysis and the New Jersey case study gives support to the literature that the actual impact of regulatory reforms is very limited. In the previous chapter, data from numerous states revealed questions about both the efficacy and the negative effects of regulatory reforms. In this chapter, those conclusions are supported by a more detailed examination of one state where regulatory reform has been a way of life.

If regulatory reform does little to affect regulatory decisions, it leaves us with a mystery. Why has there been so much regulatory reform? It is to this question that we now turn.

4 Regulations and the Economy

What we need to do is pass the mother of all repeal bills, but it's the repeal bill that will get at job killing regulations. And I would begin with the EPA, because there is no other agency like the EPA. It should really be renamed the job-killing organization of America.

Michele Bachmann (R-MN)
NH Republican Primary Debate
June 13, 2011

In the preceding two chapters, we concluded that the effect of regulatory reforms on the volume of regulations was minimal. Yet the pace of regulatory reform is only quickening. The 112th Congress considered nearly a dozen regulatory reform bills. States have been modifying their regulatory processes constantly over the past decade (Schwartz 2010). Many regulatory reforms are justified with language like the quote by Representative Michele Bachmann above.

However, if regulatory reforms do not deter regulations, then why do politicians spend the time and political capital passing and implementing them? The theories of the regulatory state discussed in Chapter One all rest upon one critical assumption. They assume that the regulations that are the output of administrative agencies have significant impacts. These impacts may be costs imposed upon businesses (or schools or hospitals or subdivisions of government) forced to comply with the regulation. The impacts may be benefits such as improved public health, worker safety, or increased fairness and equality. Political rhetoric, like that of Representative Bachmann, reinforces this perception of the critical role of regulation.

Like the theories of the regulatory state, the justification for regulatory reforms also rests upon the impact of regulations. In particular, the economic impacts are often cited as justifications for regulatory reforms. But what do we know about the effect of regulations? The answer is not as clear as politicians would like us to believe. It is not as clear as many of the theories of the administrative state assume. To understand why regulatory reform is continually pursued as a policy option, we must first discuss the impact of regulations. If regulations have the profound effects often attributed to them in the political sphere, then regulatory reforms can be understood as attempts (futile though they may be) by politicians to gain more control over them, as postulated by McNollgast and others, or to funnel the rewards of regulation to favored parties, as argued by public choice scholars and neo-pluralists. However, if the effect of regulations is more ambiguous, then we need to think more about the incentives of lawmakers who are proposing an ineffective solution to a problem that is not as big as they believe.

To be sure, the effect of regulations is a bigger subject than can be dealt with fully in two chapters of a book targeted on regulatory reforms. Our purpose in this chapter, and the one that follows, is to highlight the ambiguity that exists on this subject. In this chapter, we review the literature on the economic effect of regulations and show that there is little consensus. Then we apply our data on the number of regulations per state, and show that it does little to explain cross-state variations in economic performance.

In the next chapter we attempt to add to this data by narrowing in on five Midwestern states and looking at environmental regulations in particular. We examine both the effect of these environmental regulations in the states' economies and (through the use of a survey of business owners) the perceptions about environmental regulation. The mismatch between impacts and perceptions points us toward alternative explanations for the origins of regulatory reforms.

4.1 REGULATIONS AND BUSINESS COMPETIVENESS

While the rhetoric on the relationship between regulation and the economy has been heated in recent years,[1] the scholarly literature is much more ambiguous. Many of the efforts to explore the economic effects of regulation have been conducted at the national level. At the heart of this debate is the theory of externalities that treats natural resources as a production good; the allocation of such goods produces an external cost commonly referred to as pollution. Subsequently, control of these externalities in the form of fees, permits, and regulatory restrictions results in an economic cost to the user (Cropper and Oates 1992). Among national economies, scholars have argued that less stringent environmental policies will lead to comparative advantages for certain industries (McGuire 1982; Pethig 1979; Siebert 1977; Walley and Whitehead 1994; Yohe 1979;). This hypothesis is known as the pollution haven effect.

Throughout the 1990s, Michael E. Porter (1998) offered a rival hypothesis in several pieces of work. He summed the argument up in his comprehensive work, *The Competitive Advantage of Nations*. He attempted to refute the notion that differences in the stringency of environmental regulation explain all or most of the factors influencing business investments and location decisions. Porter found that four factors interacted to influence national competitiveness including: firm strategy, structure, and rivalry;

factor conditions (e.g., natural resources); demand conditions; and compa-rable, existing industries. He also hypothesized that environmental regula-tion produces positive effects within certain industries through technological innovation triggered by regulation. This is referred to in the literature as the Porter hypothesis (Porter and van de Linde 1995). In a subsequent empirical study Jaffe, Peterson, Portney, and Stavins (1995) cite a U.S. Environmen-tal Protection Agency (EPA) report, which concluded that "environmental regulations induce 'more cost-effective processes that both reduce emissions and the overall cost of doing business. . .' " (133).

Comparable research that also focused on the impact of environmental stringency and free trade concluded that "increases in economic activity per se need not lower environmental quality because income effects can lead to the adoption of cleaner techniques of production" (Copeland and Taylor 1994, 756). These findings were cautionary given the acknowledgment that many factors affect free trade. While Copeland and Taylor (1994) found evidence of a pollution haven effect as it relates to trade patterns, they found no evidence that it was the only variable or the one of greatest influence. Mixed results were also found in other studies where countries with rising incomes served to lower pollution (Grossman and Krueger 1991) and increases in pollution-intensive products were found in developing countries (Low and Yeats 1992). As Porter (1998) found, no single set of national conditions was favorable to all industries, which makes the task of studying the effect of stringency in environmental regulation on competitiveness more difficult; also the measure-ments of impact vary depending on the externalities, ranging from deforesta-tion and loss of habitats to air and water point-source pollution.

Jaffe et al. (1995) concluded that the relationship between environmental protection and international competitiveness lies somewhere in the middle of the theoretical debate and noted, "there is relatively little evidence to sup-port the hypothesis that environmental regulations have had a large adverse effect on competiveness. . ." (157). Moreover, they concluded the costs are relatively small as compared to other costs of doing business. These factors include differences in labor, energy and raw material expenditures, as well as the adequacy of infrastructure (Jaffe et al. 1995).

Following Jaffe's research, Miguel Quiroga, Thomas Sterner, and Martin Persson (2009) relied on output-oriented indicators, outlined in their 2009 working paper, in order to infer whether pollution havens existed in countries with lax environmental regulations. Since they believed input-oriented indi-cators captured other factors, such as environmental subsidies and stricter regulatory enforcement, they took a different approach. They hypothesized that "lax environmental regulations constitute a source of comparative advantage, causing the least-regulated countries to specialize in polluting industries," (18) and therefore have higher levels of exports than countries with environmentally stringent regulations. The results were mixed: "only in the non-metallic mineral sector is there evidence of a pollution haven" (18). In other subsectors, the opposite was found.

In recent years, studies about the effect regulations have on domestic industries have begun to emerge to supplement the cross-national studies. A number of studies have used the Clean Air Act to examine the effects of environmental regulation on employment and competitiveness within the United States. The Clean Air Act has the advantage of dividing U.S. counties into "attainment" and "non-attainment" areas for different pollutants, and requiring stricter standards for the non-attainment areas. This allows researchers to use variations in geographic and pollutant measurements to examine economic impacts.

Unfortunately, these studies have produced no more consensus than the cross-national comparisons. Morgenstern, Pizer, and Shih (2002) studied four heavily polluting industries and found that stricter environmental regulations led to greater employment in two of the industries and statistically insignificant results in the other two industries. The Environmental Protection Agency has since used this work regularly in its economic analyses to argue that the employment impacts of their regulations are negligible or positive.

Another study showing a negligible relationship between environmental stringency and employment was by Berman and Bui (2001a). They studied the effect of air quality regulations in southern California and found that there were no meaningful effects on employment. In another study of air quality in southern California, this one focusing on oil refineries, they found that productivity actually increased with more stringent regulations, and concluded that concerns about the effect of regulations on productivity were overstated (Berman and Bui 2001b).

However, numerous studies have reached opposite conclusions. The most influential of these are by Greenstone, who used extensive data on attainment and non-attainment counties over the fifteen-year period of 1972–1987. He found that a non-attainment designation cost counties 590,000 jobs, $37 billion in capital stock, and $75 billion of output in pollution-intensive industries between 1972 and 1987 (Greenstone 2002). In another work he (and his co-authors) found that non-attainment designations were associated with an approximate 2.6 percent decline in total factor productivity (Greenstone, List, and Syverson 2011). Numerous other studies have also found a negative relationship between environmental regulation and economic activity (Becker and Henderson, 2009; Gray and Shadbegian 1998; Jorgenson and Wilcoxen 1993).

Still more recent work on the relationship between environmental regulation and employment may indicate a more subtle relationship. Walker (2012) evaluates firm responses to environmental regulation at the plant level. He finds that firms are likely to respond to regulatory burdens with layoffs, and because workers in manufacturing may have trouble finding new jobs, the transition costs of unemployment for these individuals may be significant. He says, "the predominant focus of the previous literature on employment misses important aspects of labor market adjustment to environmental regulations" (30).

In a recent working paper, Sinclair and Vesey (2012) take a new approach to examining the relationship between regulation and the economy. Since many regulatory critics often cite the budgets of regulatory agencies as evidence of the reach of the regulatory state, Sinclair and Vesey examine the relationship between these budgets and both Gross Domestic Product (GDP) and employment levels. They find no appreciable relationship between GDP or employment and either aggregate spending by regulatory agencies or several disaggregated measures.

Empirical studies on the state level are even more limited. Stephen M. Meyer (1992) examined the relationship between strict environmental laws and poor economic performance. Meyer found that "at a minimum the pursuit of environmental quality does not hinder economic growth and development. Furthermore, there appears to be a moderate yet consistent positive association between environmentalism and economic growth" (as cited in Jaffe et al. 1995, 157). Still Jaffe et al. (1995) are critical of the causal assertions raised in Meyer's work because he failed to control for factors other than the stringency of a state's environmental laws.

Finally, politicians often attribute the decision to open a new plant, expand an existing plant, or shutter one to the costs of regulation. Alan M. Rugman and Alain Verbeke (2002) centered their work on corporate strategies and the "interaction between firm-level competitiveness and environmental regulations, including the conditions for the use of green capabilities" (301). They organized firms into four strategies and evaluated the conditions under which firms moved from one approach to another. This included identifying firms who went beyond "environmental excellence" and adopted environmental policies as a value-added proposition, beyond those required by regulators (Arora and Cason 1996). Rugman and Verbeke did not find empirical support for the pollution haven hypothesis and only "ambiguous conceptual support" for the Porter hypothesis. Overall, they concluded that firms have the strongest influence over their own investment strategies, and most national governments lack the resources and the power to effectuate the kinds of conditions that ultimately drive businesses to make investment decisions.

After briefly reviewing the literature on the impact of regulations on employment and economic performance, one is led to several inescapable conclusions. The first is that measuring these impacts is hard. We don't mean this to be glib. There is considerable theoretical appeal to the argument that regulations that restrict the behavior of business owners will lead to lower employment and reduce their competitiveness. Generally, decisions by business owners to hire or fire workers are influenced by many factors including the overall economy, the cost of health care, laws such as minimum wages, and the ability to find quality workers. With all of these interrelated parts, the effect of regulation is hard to isolate. In most cases, the effect of regulation is likely to be smaller than these other effects, making its detection even more difficult.

Second, the extant research on regulations and the economy is ambiguous.[2] Some studies show the predicted effects (Greenstone 2002) while others show insignificant effects of regulation on employment levels or even positive ones (Morgenstern, Pizer, and Shih 2002). Scholars on both sides of the debate acknowledge that the effects of regulation may differ when the economy is healthy (and there is "full employment") and displaced workers can easily find other jobs and when the economy is in recession and long terms of unemployment may be more common (Davis and von Wachter 2011). A recent issue brief from the Wharton School (Coglianese 2013) summed this ambiguity up, "The empirical research, although limited . . . fails to support the notion that regulation is either a major job killer or significant job creator" (5).

This ambiguity and nuance differs sharply from the political rhetoric on the subject. The phrase "job-killing regulations" has become part of the political discourse. One study reports a 17,550 percent increase of the phrase in the media between 2007 and 2011 (Livermore, Piennar, and Schwartz 2012). This prevalence far exceeds the research supporting the idea that regulations kill jobs.

Yet the effects of regulations on jobs and other economic variables certainly merit further examination. As Masur and Posner (2012) point out, recent research on the costs of unemployment, and the difficulty of finding a new job during the Great Recession, make it imperative to understand whether regulation impacts employment. Further, understanding these effects enlighten the debate on regulatory reform. In Chapters Two and Three we cast doubt on the efficacy of regulatory procedures. The most frequent justification for these reforms is that they will help the economy (particularly employment) by curbing regulation.[3] We've already concluded that regulatory reforms do little to curb regulation. If curbing regulation will have little impact on the economy, a further piece of the justification for regulatory reforms is eliminated.

Unfortunately but not unsurprisingly, as we describe below, our state data is unable to cast much additional light on this complicated question. Rather, our data reinforces the two conclusions described above about understanding this relationship. Doing so is complicated and the effects of regulation are likely to be ambiguous and vary from issue to issue. This may also support Walker's (2012) argument that economic effects of regulation are not seen in aggregate numbers but rather in changes in individual plants and costly transitions for individual workers. This more specific effect has important implications for the politics of regulatory reform.

4.2 OUR DATA

In Chapter Two, we used the number of rules issued in twenty-eight states in calendar year 2007 as a dependent variable. In theory, our collection of this data presents an excellent opportunity to examine the relationship between regulatory volume and the economy. For the first time we can compare the number of regulations in a state with indicators representing the health of the state economies. Do states with more regulations exhibit weaker economic performance?

However, there are two significant problems with this approach. First, as the literature above indicates, regulatory effects on the macro economy, if they exist, are likely to be obscured by other more significant factors. With a dataset that has only twenty-eight observations, we do not have the ability to run a regression model and include all the variables that would likely have larger economic impacts than regulation.

Second, the lagged impact of regulations probably varies considerably over different policy areas. Regulations often take time to go into effect and then, even once they are in effect, it may be some time before their impacts are felt. We attempt to deal with this issue in Chapter Five by looking at regulatory levels over a multiyear period in five Midwestern states. However, it is a significant limitation on our ability to draw conclusions from the one year of data presented in this chapter.

Acknowledging these limitations, it is still useful to present the data on regulatory volume and economic output for 2007. We will be circumspect in drawing conclusions from this data, instead relying on the literature cited above to describe the economic impact of regulation as ambiguous. As shown below, our data is also ambiguous.

Independent Variable—How Many Rules?

In this chapter, our independent variable is now the data on the number of rules that we collected from twenty-eight states and used in Chapter Two as a dependent variable. Here again, we also broke out the number of rules that were budgetary or administrative in nature and excluded them from the analysis, creating a variable we called "economic rules." For further detail on the "total rules" and "economic rules" variables, we refer the reader to Chapter Two.

Our justification for using total rules (or total number of economic rules) to represent regulatory burden is the same as it was in Chapter Two. Much of the debate about regulation focuses on the sheer number of rules issued by agencies, making an examination of the impact of regulatory volume on economic indicators a legitimate question (in our survey in Chapter Five, the overall number of regulations also jumps out as a significant concern for business owners). Further, as previously described, regulatory volume has a strong correlation with independent measures of the "freedom" in the states, giving it further legitimacy (Sorens and Ruger 2009).

That is not to say that it is a perfect instrument for capturing regulatory burden. Rules can be regulatory or deregulatory in nature, and presumably deregulatory actions should have the opposite effect on the economy (and on public health) as regulatory ones. Counting the number of rules obscures this difference, and this may be particularly important as the category of rules gets smaller (from all rules with an economic impact to just environmental rules). Further, one rule with a very significant economic impact may outweigh dozens of other rules. We are conscious of these limitations and will qualify our conclusions appropriately. We also address this issue by examining environmental regulation in five states in more detail in Chapter Five.

Measurements of Economic Output and Quality of Life

In choosing dependent variables, we focused on the economic factors that are most often cited as being detrimentally affected by regulations. We assume that changes in these factors are the ones that political actors will respond to by enacting regulatory reforms. First and foremost of course is the effect of regulations on jobs, which has been at the center of recent political debates over regulation. Our first metric of economic health is the unemployment rate. We found the unemployment rates in 2007 and the year-to-year changes at the U.S. Bureau of Labor Statistics (2007b).

Regulations are also often blamed for their burden on small businesses. To examine the small business climates in the twenty-eight states in our dataset, we utilized a variety of measures from the U.S. Census Bureau. These include business start-ups and business failures, which were collected from the 2007 Statistics of U.S. Businesses (SUSB) Data. Census data was also used to capture population per state, which in turn was used to transform some outcome measures into per capita variables.

To gain further insights into the variations among the states, we recorded the minimum wage, published by the U.S. Bureau of Labor Statistics (BLS) (2007a). Of note, 58.5 percent of all wage and salary workers were paid at hourly rates in 2007, according to the Current Population Survey. The minimum wage was also raised from $5.15 an hour to $5.85 an hour in August of 2007.

To examine the overall economy of a state, several variables were used: per capita state Gross Domestic Product (GDP), changes in state GDP from 2006 to 2007 (Copeland and Taylor 1994, 2004; Jaffe et al. 1995), and median household income and state personal income in 2007 (Grossman and Krueger 1991; Copeland and Taylor 1994). The Per Capita Personal Income was also collected by the BLS (2007c); it is different from national personal income in that the Census Bureau only counts the income of those persons living within that state, including foreign residents in the latter reference. State Median Income was collected by the Census Bureau, and it represents the three-year median of inflation-adjusted single-year medians. The Department of Commerce Bureau of Economic Analysis (2007) was our source for GDP by state and for changes in the rate from 2006 to 2007.

4.3 ANALYSIS

Regulations and Small Businesses

Among the most frequent arguments voiced by critics of government regulations is that they inhibit small businesses. Below, we show a comparison of the number of regulations promulgated in 2007 with business start-ups in 2007 and business deaths in 2007. If the critics are correct, then more regulations should mean fewer start-ups and more businesses shutting their doors.

It is plausible that there would be a time lag between a regulatory surge and an impact on small businesses. We did not use data from years later than 2007 for two reasons. First, the effects of the recession that began in 2008 were likely to swamp any impacts due to regulations (even more than the other factors in the economy mentioned above). Second, we are confident that our data (both regulatory and economic) in 2007 are not anomalous. If a state issued a large number of regulations in 2007, it is likely that it regularly issues many regulations.[4]

The correlation coefficient between the number of regulations issued and the number of start-ups was positive but was not statistically significant. States that issued more regulations saw more businesses come into being in 2007 (dividing the sample into states with more than the median number of regulations and states with fewer); high-regulation states had 359 start-ups per 100,000 inhabitants and low-regulation states had 319 start-ups per 100,000 inhabitants. However, the difference was not statistically significant.

Controlling for the tax burden on businesses in each state did not substantially alter the results. When we controlled for the minimum wage, we can see how the impacts of regulation can often be obscured by more important variables as described above. Table 4.1 shows the number of start-ups per 100,000 inhabitants for states above and below the median number of regulations and minimum wage.

While the trend for more start-ups in high regulation states continues regardless of the minimum wage, the relationship between start-ups and the minimum wage is as traditionally predicted (Card and Kreuger 1997): The higher the minimum wage, the fewer the number of start-ups. This finding is also in line with other scholars who hypothesize that other factors—other than regulations—influence firm strategies (Porter 1998; Jaffe et al. 1995; Rugman and Verbeke 2002).

Table 4.1 Business Start-ups (per 100,000 Inhabitants) and Regulatory Volume

	High Minimum Wage States	Low Minimum Wage States
High Regulatory Volume	340	377
Low Regulatory Volume	303	333

Table 4.2 Business Deaths (per 100,000 Inhabitants) and Regulatory Volume

	High Minimum Wage States	Low Minimum Wage States
High Regulatory Volume	273	249
Low Regulatory Volume	251	286

Regulations are often cited as a cause of business failures. So in addition to looking at business start-ups, we looked at business failures. The correlation between business deaths and regulations was not statistically significant. "High-regulation states" (those with more than the median number of regulations issued in 2007) had 268 business deaths per 100,000 inhabitants and low-regulation states had 260 business deaths per 100,000 inhabitants.

Again, no additional information was gained by controlling for the tax burden on businesses. Finally, we examined the relationship between regulation, minimum wage, and business failures. The results are presented in Table 4.2.

The results here are not revealing, as states with high minimum wages and a high level of regulations have a higher number of business deaths, but so do states with low minimum wages and low regulatory output.

Regulations and the Economy

To listen to the political rhetoric (see the Rep. Michele Bachmann quote at the beginning of this chapter), it is not just small businesses that suffer because of regulations; it is the economy as a whole. We looked at the relationship between regulatory output and a series of indicators described above meant to represent the economic health of the state.

As described above, there are significant limitations to our ability to draw conclusions from this data. Even if this data were perfect, however, only two

Table 4.3 Correlations among Economic Measures and Regulatory Volume

Variable	Correlation Coefficient with Regulatory Output (*statistically significant)
Unemployment	0.02
Change in Unemployment (2006–07)	0.07
GDP per Capita	0.29
Change in GDP per Capita	0.30
Median Household Income	0.33*
State Personal Income	0.40*

Note: $p < 0.05$*

of the relationships show statistical significance, and this is in the opposite direction from that hypothesized by critics of regulation. And for these two variables (median household income and personal income), it strikes us that the direction of causality is not clear. Citizens in more prosperous states may very well demand more regulation than citizens in less prosperous states. Prosperity is at least as likely to cause high levels of regulation as regulation is to cause higher levels of prosperity. We have no means of detecting the direction of causality.

In short, our data on state regulatory output and state economic performance add little to the understanding of the relationship between regulation and the economy in the more sophisticated studies that have preceded our work. As we said at the outset, the magnitude of the rhetoric about "job-killing" regulations is likely overblown.

4.4 DISCUSSION

The justification most often cited for regulatory reform is that regulations harm the economy and reforms are a way to either produce less costly regulations (in the case of reforms requiring analysis) or regulations that better reflect the popular will (in the case of reforms that require political review or participation). However, the political rhetoric is far ahead of the evidence on the relationship between regulation and the economy.

As described above, the literature that has examined the relationships between regulation and economic variables has not produced definitive results. Some studies have shown the relationship predicted by most theorists. Regulation has been shown to have a negative effect on employment (Greenstone 2002) and productivity (Jorgenson and Wilcoxen 1993). These studies give support to the critics of regulation and therefore the supporters of regulatory reform.

Still, there have also been numerous studies that show an ambiguous (or even a positive) relationship between regulation and key economic variables. This is true both for employment (Morgenstern, Pizer, and Shih 2002) and for productivity (Berman and Bui 2001b). These and other studies support the hypothesis that regulation also has positive economic effects (Porter 1998), and they thereby weaken the case for regulatory reform. Coglianese (2013) sums up the ambiguity by saying, "Based on the existing empirical evidence, U.S. policy-makers should not expect that the nation's economic woes can be solved by reforming the regulatory process" (5).

Our state data are similarly ambiguous. The volume of regulation in the states has no correlation with business start-ups or business closings. It has no relationship with the unemployment rate, which deflates the most frequently stated claim about the harm of regulation and the justification for regulatory reform. While it appears to be correlated with several other measures of economic well-being, the direction of causality is likely to run in the opposite direction. States with more prosperous populations are more likely to demand higher levels of regulation.

And yet the sentiment that regulation harms the economy is a persistent one. There are two possible reasons for this persistence. One is that while regulations may not have measurable impacts on aggregate levels of employment or economic well-being, they may have a large effect on very small populations. Recent work by Walker (2012) raises this possibility, and Masur and Posner (2012) highlight the possible economic significance of these effects.

The fact that regulations have impacts that are not broad enough to affect the general economy, even at the state level, but have acute effects at the individual level has important implications for the political motivations behind regulatory reform. Political science literature emphasizes that when the costs of a policy are concentrated and the benefits are diffuse, those bearing the costs will be given disproportionate attention (Wilson 1980). This could explain why politicians are eager to create mechanisms to influence particular regulations.

Regulations are often targeted at particular industries or collections of industries. Pollution-control requirements hit hardest on the chemical and manufacturing sectors. Worker safety rules are often targeted on industries with particular hazards. If regulations lead to job losses in these sectors, then this may merit attention. While regulation may not raise the unemployment rate, that is little consolation to those who have lost their jobs and, fairly or not, blame regulation. Regulatory reforms may be an attempt to create a means for politicians to intervene in particular regulatory decisions and help this concentrated constituency.

The other possible explanation is a more cynical one. The Bachmann quote at the outset of this chapter was not chosen accidentally. Politicians are often judged on economic conditions when they are in office. However, individual officeholders have little influence over the overall economy. Instead, the temptation exists to find a culprit for a poor economy. Time and again over the past several decades, regulation has proven an attractive target.

It makes intuitive sense that regulation harms the economy. Regulation certainly restricts choices of businesses, and in doing so it engenders the resentment of those businesses. However, once politicians blame regulations for economic conditions, they need to produce a solution for this regulatory problem. And they need to do so without angering the sizeable constituencies that support regulation. Perhaps this is why regulatory reform is so popular, particularly in poorer economic times.

To attempt to understand these possible justifications for regulatory reforms, the next chapter looks at one sector of regulations (environmental) in five states. This multiple case study approach is intended to add depth to the understanding of the relationship between regulation and the economy in these states. It also examines the perceptions of business owners in these five states. These dual, detailed examinations of both actual and perceived impacts give further support to the above explanations for the passage of regulatory reforms.

5 Seeing Red

Are Regulations a Perceived or Actual Threat?

Does regulation make a difference in the economy? Is less government—restrained by fewer regulations—better government, or is more regulation necessary for a modern economy? While the literature we reviewed in the previous chapter invites a robust debate, there appears to be no clear relationship between regulation and macroeconomic conditions. However, before reaching any definitive conclusions, we believe that looking more closely at a smaller number of jurisdictions may prove helpful.

We begin by trying to understand the states (or at least some states) in more detail. Rather than examining relationships over twenty-eight states, in this chapter, we examine the relationship between regulatory volume and economic conditions in five Midwestern states. We take an empirical look at the relationship between economic and environmental regulations and macroeconomic factors in the region. Then, we explore the question of how the regulated community perceives regulation. Toward this end, we talked to business owners within these states to discern their perceptions about regulation. If the data on the impact of regulation does not explain the need for regulatory reform, perhaps the perception of regulation does.

There is considerable evidence of a widely held perception that regulation hurts the economy. In researching Chapter Seven, we talked to a business leader in North Carolina who told us with confidence that the blame for the anticompetitive business climate and the poor economy in his state was due to the number of regulations that exist. Referring to the prior administration he said, "We had a regulation producing machine. Government went unchecked."

Likewise, the role of regulation was a central pivot point differentiating the two major party candidates in the 2012 presidential campaign. Regulations were criticized as "killing jobs" and hurting the economy by Republican challenger Mitt Romney, who squarely endorsed the principle that "less government is better government."[1] In a speech delivered on the national economy in Iowa during the waning days of the campaign, Romney targeted regulations as part of the reason President Barack Obama had failed to create "essential growth and employment" in the private sector. In Romney's remarks, he focused his criticisms by asserting:

He [Obama] launched an onslaught of new regulations, often to the delight of the biggest banks and corporations, but to the detriment of the small, growing businesses that create two-thirds of our jobs. New business starts are at a 30-year low because entrepreneurs and investors are sitting on the sidelines, weary from the President's staggering new regulations and proposed massive tax increases.[2]

As explained earlier, claims about the economic impact of regulations are backed by limited evidence. While it is not unusual in the political arena to exaggerate the evidence for a claim, the level of ambiguity about regulatory impacts on jobs is unusually high. In the numerous cross-national studies and studies of the domestic economy, the conclusions have been largely ambiguous. In order to more closely examine whether regulatory burden hurts the economy and businesses, we compiled a unique dataset of environmental regulations in five states over a period of seven years (the maximum number of years for which data were available). Our purpose in Chapter Five is to focus our examination on a particular type of regulation in order to better understand both actual and perceived regulatory impacts.

Environmental regulations were selected for several reasons. In many instances, federal environmental regulations are left to the states to implement or monitor. The states are often governed by similar environmental parameters; yet some state policy-makers seek to adopt regulations that are more stringent than the federal rules, just as others consider federal mandates to be the ceiling for state rulemaking. Environmental policies are typically viewed as the most costly regulations to comply with, and they are often cited as the kind of regulations that business leaders "seriously agree" are of the most concern to them (and Governor Romney's rhetoric on the campaign trail often focused on environmental regulations). Finally, environmental regulations are regularly regarded by policy-makers and stakeholders alike as the most controversial and complex rules to implement. Hence it is in this policy area that we would expect the perception about the negative impacts of regulation to be the strongest.

5.1 OUR DATA

To choose our states, we first identified adjacent states that had variation in the number of regulations adopted annually, as this serves as our key independent variable of study (see Table 5.1). Variation in the independent variable is a well-recognized method for selecting cases in multi-case studies (King, Keohane, and Verba 1994). We also wanted states within the same geographic region to control for economic conditions that vary by region of the country and to control for possible policy diffusion effects (Walker 1969).

Table 5.1 Comparison of Laws to Economic and Environmental Regulations

State	Year	Total Laws	Env. Laws	Total Rules	Economic Rules	Env. Rules
Illinois	2003	577	22			
Illinois	2004	525	15			
Illinois	2005	414	22	480	261	50
Illinois	2006	642	11	450	236	41
Illinois	2007	256	32	381	187	39
Illinois	2008	800	3	423	212	32
Illinois	2009	800	14	358	195	24
Illinois	2010	699	24	360	196	40
Illinois	2011	649	7	444	237	39
Total		5362	150	2896	1524	265
Indiana	2003	280	2			
Indiana	2004	98	1			
Indiana	2005	231	3	225	100	51
Indiana	2006	194	4	253	118	37
Indiana	2007	234	0	218	60	29
Indiana	2008	147	4	338	167	47
Indiana	2009	182	14	263	100	27
Indiana	2010	116	0	280	90	29
Indiana	2011	231	3	258	92	31
Total		1713	31	1835	727	251
Michigan	2003	322	1			
Michigan	2004	596	6			
Michigan	2005	340	4	56	53	12
Michigan	2006	682	2	66	61	11
Michigan	2007	221	12	64	58	6
Michigan	2008	586	3	46	43	11
Michigan	2009	242	0	46	40	18
Michigan	2010	348	9	37	37	23
Michigan	2011	323	2	40	40	4
Total		3660	39	355	332	85
Minnesota	2003	156	2			
Minnesota	2004	162	0			
Minnesota	2005	177	0	61	37	7
Minnesota	2006	113	1	63	28	4
Minnesota	2007	220	6	72	36	4
Minnesota	2008	152	3	74	38	11
Minnesota	2009	179	5	72	37	5

Continued

Table 5.1 Continued

State	Year	Total Laws	Env. Laws	Total Rules	Economic Rules	Env. Rules
Minnesota	2010	222	15	56	24	2
Minnesota	2011	129	1	71	39	4
Total		1510	33	469	239	37
Wisconsin	2003	111	3			
Wisconsin	2004	216	0			
Wisconsin	2005	77	0	150	113	39
Wisconsin	2006	415	2	118	80	19
Wisconsin	2007	42	0	134	99	27
Wisconsin	2008	200	2	112	72	16
Wisconsin	2009	100	0	88	64	10
Wisconsin	2010	306	9	159	112	26
Wisconsin	2011	286	0	74	57	10
Total		1753	16	835	597	147

We were limited of course by the fact that we had data on regulatory volume for just over half of the states. This narrowed our ability to select multiple states within numerous regions of the country. We had data on several states in the Midwest, however. We collected data in the following Midwestern states (hereafter referred to as the region): Illinois (IL), Indiana (IN), Michigan (MI) Minnesota (MN), and Wisconsin (WI).[3] Each state shares two contiguous borders with the other states in the region, with the exception of Minnesota, which only borders one state.

Our longitudinal design covers the period from 2005 through 2011. Collectively these five states make up 13 percent of the U.S. population and 13.7 percent of the country's nonfarm establishment employment in 2010. The firms in this region reported by the U.S. Bureau of Labor Statistics in 2007 made 18.5 percent of all manufacturing shipments in the country, along with 13.1 percent of all merchant wholesaler sales and 12.7 percent of all retail sales. Because our policy focus is on environmental regulations, we wanted to ensure our selection comprised states that were typical of U.S. commerce and included a robust manufacturing sector. Additionally, the political landscape of the region is not shaded by one-party dominance.

Before we assess whether a correlation exists between economic conditions and the number of environmental regulations, we first describe the political climate in the region, and take a look at the actions of the state legislatures in these states in an attempt to further understand the role that laws play in the volume of regulation in a state. We then supplement our empirical findings on regulatory impacts with findings on perception of regulatory impacts by reporting on a random survey of business leaders in these five states designed to learn what they believe about the correlation between regulations and the burden on their businesses.

5.2 THE FIVE MIDWESTERN STATES

Not surprisingly, given the backdrop of the national economic slowdown at the time, the rhetorical debate about the effects of government regulations was quite prominent in these five states. When we asked regional business leaders whether reducing the number of regulations was the best way to create jobs in the U.S. in early 2013, we found half of those surveyed (49 percent) shared this belief while others believed the number of regulations was not the biggest factor influencing their businesses (49 percent). Still, we did find wide variations between the states—with 62 percent of executives in Indiana agreeing with the contention that reducing regulations was an optimal economic stimulus as compared to 38 percent of business leaders in Michigan. We return to this discussion later in this chapter, but first, it is helpful to understand the politics during this period in the five states.

In Wisconsin, there was no partisan divide when it came to the need to promote economic recovery during the 2010 campaign. For both major party candidates, there was a focus on reducing and streamlining regulations during the open seat election. Mayor Thomas Barrett (D), unsuccessfully vied for the previously held Democratic seat against Republican Scott Walker. According to an online position paper, "Creating Jobs for Wisconsin," Candidate Barrett promised to, "simplify regulations and streamline the regulatory process to lighten the burden on business without sacrificing protections of workers, families and our environment" if elected. Similarly, Walker, who won the election, also vowed to realign Wisconsin's regulatory regime. Walker spotlighted those early efforts in his most recent State of the State address, delivered on January 15, 2013:

> Last year, I called for state agencies to work with the reformed Small Business Regulatory Review Board to identify unnecessary, obsolete, and burdensome regulations. We asked employers what we can do to help them create jobs and the most common answer was decrease the amount of regulations.[4]

The governor has also proposed a regulatory reform measure that diminishes the budget of bureaucracies, while increasing the government's oversight over its actions.

During the same 2010 campaign cycle, a similar battle was being waged across the lake in Michigan. Republican business executive Rick Snyder faced off against Democratic Mayor Virgil Bernero for the open seat previously held by a Democrat. Here as well, there was little distinction between the candidates when it came to the steps each offered to take to reduce regulatory burden. Upon his election, Governor Snyder pursued a more surgical approach towards reform by "modernizing" rather than eliminating regulations.[5] Snyder's executive order established the Department of Insurance and Financial Services, which was charged with the tasks of promoting efficient and effective regulations within the financial, insurance, and banking industries, one of the state's largest business sectors. Snyder tied his reform efforts to his belief that modernizing state regulations helps eliminate barriers to job growth. In issuing the order, Snyder proclaimed:

> By establishing a new department dedicated to industry sustainability it further emphasizes the commitment to removing red tape from economic growth in Michigan. This order will also go a long way toward creating and enforcing appropriate regulations.[6]

In Minnesota, another gubernatorial contest for an open seat was also taking place in 2010 between U.S. Senator Mark Dayton (MN-DFL)[7] and Tom Elmer (R), a Representative in the Minnesota legislature. In a press release touting Elmer's proposed budget plan, he claimed he would "put state government bureaucracies on a diet" by "cut[ting] bureaucracies and programs that are not fundamental to state government's mission (http://www.emmerforgovernor.com/news/2010/09/emmer-budget-plan-part-3-government-reform.html)." Elmer also wrote that "Onerous regulations that frustrate employers and destroy jobs must be dismantled to allow growth" (http://emmerforgovernor.com/issues/smallbusiness/). By contrast, Governor Dayton's regulatory reforms have been more moderate and seem reflective of the perspectives held by business leaders today, who are split down the middle on the question of whether deregulation helps to create jobs. Dayton's approach focused on streamlining business permitting and licensing through the creation of online processes. Here the chief executive's goals stop short of eliminating government rules while shifting the emphasis towards improving the delivery of state government services.

The 2010 campaign for Illinois governor was waged between State Senator Bill Brady (R) and Pat Quinn (D). As the former lieutenant governor, Quinn was the incumbent, having filled the unexpired term of Governor Rod Blagojevich, who resigned in 2009. While both campaign rivals offered plans to stimulate the economy and aid small businesses, this is the only state in the region where neither candidate focused on specific regulatory reforms. No doubt the federal corruption indictment of former Governor Blagojevich, coupled with a looming state budget deficit, converged to shift the focus of Governor Quinn towards raising ethical standards and cutting the size of government.

More recently in 2012 and to the south in Indiana, a battle was waged for another open gubernatorial seat between two long-term politicians:

Republican Representative Mike Pence (IN-2) and the Democratic Speaker of the Indiana House of Representative, John Gregg. Gregg focused on making the state a leader in the agriculture, advanced manufacturing, energy, logistics, and life sciences industries in order to strengthen the state's economy. Gregg also argued that long-term growth would require streamlining of business regulations through the use of comprehensive rulemaking reforms, including cost-benefit analysis.

Governor Pence, who assumed the reins from a previous Republican governor, quickly sought to limit the number of regulations on businesses. In his State of the State address delivered on January 22, 2013 he explained:

> It all starts by making job creation job one. That's why on day one of our administration, I signed a moratorium on any new regulations to ensure that Indiana is not burdening Hoosier employers with unnecessary red tape.[8]

Pence believes that his Administration's review of current regulations and the removal of regulatory barriers will promote an increase in private sector employment and attract new investments, and a higher quality workforce.

What this examination of the regional political culture illuminates are two observations. First, regulatory reforms appear to gain attention from policymakers and prospective statewide candidates when their state economies are challenged by recession. This pattern likely stems from a desire to blame the poor economy on something. Regulation provides an outstanding target both because candidates may feel it is a problem they can do something about once in office and because there may be a legitimate concern about the effects of regulation that are heightened under depressed economic conditions (Davis and von Wachter 2011).

We also saw this pattern of focusing on regulation during difficult economic times in New Jersey in Chapter Three, and it will appear again in the examinations of Pennsylvania and North Carolina in Chapter Seven. Absent this economic pressure, regulations and regulatory reforms received much less attention, as demonstrated by the absence of gubernatorial executive orders issued targeting regulatory reforms and the lack of prominence given to regulation in annual State of the State addresses prior to the onset of the Great Recession in 2008 in these states. On its face, regulatory reform seems like a peculiar response to the argument that regulations negatively impact states' economies and businesses. If regulations impose negative consequences, one would expect the political rhetoric to be constantly infused with calls for a solution that works rather than for regulatory reforms, which have at best ambiguous impacts.[9]

Second, it appears that Republican executives more regularly highlighted the impact of government regulations as compared to Democratic governors in this region. In Wisconsin, Governor Walker even commissioned a survey asking employers to identify "unnecessary, obsolete and burdensome regulations."[10] Even in the aftermath of the recession, Democrats were a bit more guarded when it came to the notion that government regulations produced mostly negative effects. The exception is Governor Snyder, who according to reported accounts does not always reflect across-the-board Republican Party positions. We will examine these party effects in greater detail in Chapter Six.

5.3 A LOOK AT LEGISLATIVE DEMAND

Before examining how regulations impact the economy in these five states, we use the advantages of a multiple-state case study to shed more light on one of our findings in Chapter Two. Recall, we did not see a significant relationship between the volume of lawmaking and that of rulemaking in our national cross-sectional analysis. Yet this review had limitations: Across twenty-eight states, the relationship between laws and regulations could vary considerably. We could not delve into the substance of the laws, many of which were likely ceremonial, over such a large body of states. Similarly, we could not determine how long after a passage of a law an agency would promulgate a "mandatory" rule required by that statute.

In Chapter Two, we determined that political party (particularly control of the legislature) had more to do with the production of regulations than the presence or absence of regulatory reforms. We hypothesized that this was because Democratic legislatures produced more laws that required agency regulations than Republican ones. This is important, because if regulation is largely due to laws, then regulatory reform (even if it works) is an inefficient way to reduce regulation. Politicians wanting to eliminate regulations should repeal the laws that produce them.

We re-examine this question here in the Midwest, both for environmental regulations and for all regulations with an economic impact. We do so with the hope that by looking at a particular policy area and by looking at a smaller number of states over time, we can better understand the relationship between laws passed and regulations promulgated.

Two-Stage Analysis

First, we examined the relationship between the volume of lawmaking and the total number of regulations, as well as the kinds of regulations adopted annually in the states. For this first level of analysis, we compare total laws to total economic rules (as defined in Chapter Two); as well as total environmental laws enacted to total environmental rules adopted. Figures 5.1 and 5.2 display how we aggregated the data.

Over the past twelve years, we also see little evidence to suggest there has been a retreat in the kind of environmental laws adopted by state legislatures. Based on an analysis of data compiled by the National Conference of State

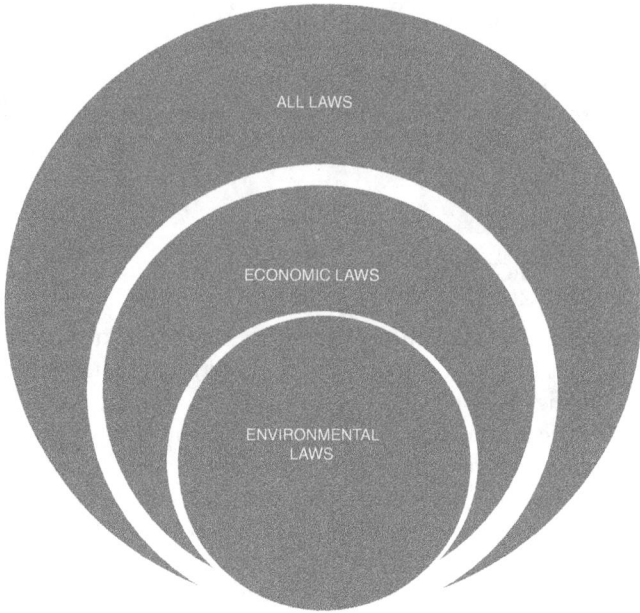

Figure 5.1

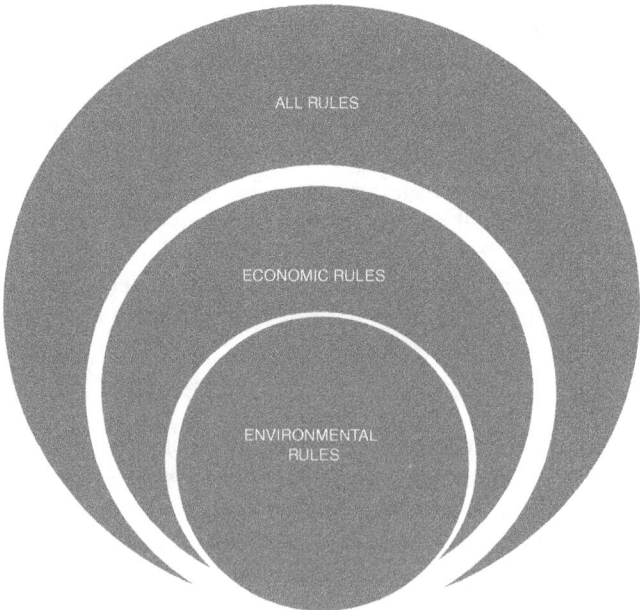

Figure 5.2

Note: Each circle contains categories of laws or rules. The smaller concentric circles include a precisely defined category, while each wider concentric circle is all inclusive and represents a broader category of rules or laws.

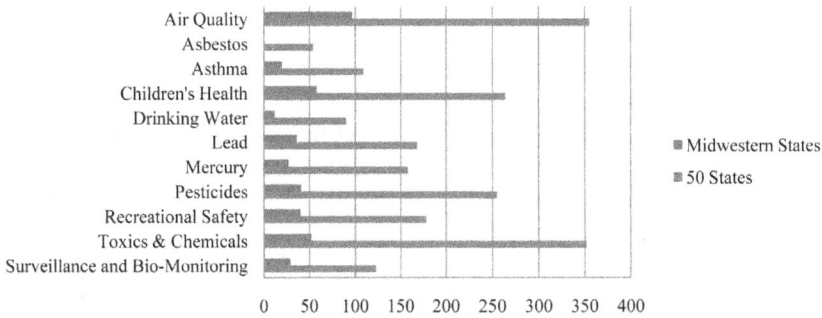

Figure 5.3 Environmental Laws Adopted (2001–2012)

Legislatures (NCSL), the number of environmental laws adopted from 2001 through 2012 totaled 2106. These laws focused on a broad array of activities, as displayed in Figure 5.3.The Midwestern states in our regional study adopted a large proportion of these laws, totaling 412 statutes or 20 percent of the overall environmental laws enacted across the country. Clear differences emerge in the type of environmental laws adopted in the Midwest as compared to other states. For example, as shown in Figure 5.3, Midwestern states enacted a disproportionate share of air quality and children's health laws while not enacting any laws on asbestos contamination. These variations can in part be explained by the differences in political culture and the local economies.

Each state has its own individual regional economy. Determinants of a state's economic drivers include but are not limited to the physical infrastructure, human resources, tax and regulation, capital finance, and the technology research and development environment existing within the state. From a regional perspective, there are not significant variations by sectors, although there is variation in the total number of business establishments among the states, which likely produces an influence on public policy.[11]

While there are differences in the state economies, the states are home to a robust manufacturing sector, which serves as one of the top three employers in each of the states.

In addition to differences in the economies, political differences can influence the types of laws enacted. Over this period, there was a steady change in governance occurring. Split legislatures existed over half the years, while partisan divisions between the executive and legislative branches occurred nearly a quarter of the time. More specifically, every state had a divided legislative chamber during this period and three of the five states, Minnesota, Michigan, and Wisconsin, had divided branches of government.

Stage One

With this background, we present the volume of lawmaking as compared to the volume of regulations over the seven-year period. For this analysis, we lag the data since the influence (laws enacted) is expected to occur in a session year that precedes the rulemaking calendar year by one to two years in most cases.

What is immediately apparent is that the total volume of lawmaking dwarfs the total volume of rulemaking when the years are lagged in every state but Indiana. When the laws are lagged by one year, the ratio of total laws to total regulations is: 1.4 (IL), 0.7 (IN), 8.5 (MI), 2.6 (MN), and 1.6 (WI). Lawmaking activities, relative to rulemaking, are greatest in Michigan while most limited in Minnesota. When the laws are lagged by two years, we see almost identical results: 1.4 (IL), 0.7 (IN), 8.4 (MI), 2.5 (MN), and 1.4 (WI). We find a statistically significant relationship (at the 1 percent level) between the total number of laws and the total number of regulations with a two-year lag (correlation coefficient = 0.437). There is a slightly weaker association when the data is lagged by one year.

While the correlation between environmental laws and environmental regulations is statistically significant (at the 5 percent level) when lagged by two years, this association disappears when the data is lagged by only one year (correlation coefficient = 0.401). This could be because environmental statutes have less strict deadlines for rule promulgation than other statutes, that environmental laws require more complex and hence time-consuming regulations than other statutes, or that more environmental regulation is discretionary in nature.

Also of interest is that while the total number of laws exceeds the total number of regulations, the same is not true when both variables are limited to environmental policy. This could be an artifact of our data collection process (since we focused on picking out environmental statutes, there are no merely ceremonial statutes in the number of environmental laws). It could also be due to the complexity of environmental policy, meaning that each statute naturally leads to multiple regulations. Or it could be because environmental agencies use their discretion to issue more rules.

Overall, the significant correlations between laws and regulations support the notion that direct legislative demand is correlated to the volume of rulemaking taking place when you look at these relationships over time. Still, it does not explain what is happening in Indiana. Here it very well may be the case that the higher number of regulations as compared to new laws is being caused by factors besides legislative demand. Alternatively, it may mean more legislative delegation is occurring due to the low volume of lawmaking taking place or that each law in Indiana requires more regulations. This invites the second stage of analysis. We felt the need to further explore the degree to which environmental laws appear to invite discretionary regulations.

Stage Two

In the second stage of analysis, we look for evidence of agency discretion by dividing the total environmental rules adopted annually into two regulatory products: mandatory regulations and discretionary regulations. We have defined mandatory regulations as those rules derived from laws enacted during the prior two-year period and discretionary regulations as those rule-making actions initiated pursuant to much older statutes. Because this level of analysis required a time-consuming process of detailed coding for each regulation, we focused our study on environmental regulations adopted in one state, Michigan, during the study period, focusing exclusively on those rules that added requirements as compared to rules that may have been deregulatory in nature (n = 48).

What we found may be unique to Michigan, but it was nonetheless revealing. None of the regulations we reviewed dealing with air and water quality standards as well as emission standards were linked to statutes that had been enacted into law in the prior two-year period. In fact, one regulation cited its authority as arising from a 1916 statute, while most others were tied to laws that had been enacted more than ten, and up to forty years prior. In some instances, regulatory authority was also sourced to multiple code citations as well as executive orders. While recent environmental laws have been enacted, as displayed in Table 5.1, what we see is that the broad majority of environmental regulatory activity stems from statutes enacted more than two years prior to the issuance of the regulation.

This suggests several possibilities. First, environmental regulation may indeed be a unique case. Those stakeholders we interviewed in the states often cited environmental regulations as the most complex and controversial kinds of rules. Like three of the other states in the region,[12] Michigan prescribes a time period in which a regulation must be adopted from the time it is proposed; this may invite agency personnel to delay in initiating an environmental rulemaking procedure until bureaucrats have drafted, vetted, and fine-tuned the proposal. It also suggests that lawmakers may delegate wider powers to agencies on controversial and complex environmental laws that then trigger future regulatory actions for years to come.[13] Under these conditions, one law has the potential of generating a series of regulations in the years following enactment. Pass a statute with broad delegations and future coalitions will be unable to halt rulemaking with procedural constraints (although they can still decline to take advantage of the delegation).

Ideally, future research should seek to differentiate among the causes of discretionary rulemaking; to what extent are discretionary regulations the result of endogenous changes, legislative delegation, or bureaucratic overreach. By determining this root cause, which is likely to vary by state, policy-makers can more directly focus their efforts on reforms intended to curtail the number of regulations. Likewise, the public and regulated community will be better informed as to where to target their attention: at the feet of prolific lawmakers or the agency bureaucrats who produce discretionary regulations, or both.

This analysis yields the conclusion that the passage of new laws is a significant factor in the number of regulations in the region. Even still, as the analysis of environmental regulation in Michigan suggests, it is probably not the only factor. While the volume of lawmaking does not explain all of the variation in regulatory volume, it does suggest that if regulations do affect the economy, or if they are perceived to affect the economy, legislators should look in the mirror when assigning responsibility. Now we return to the question of the actual and perceived effects of regulation.

5.4 REGULATIONS AND THE MIDWEST ECONOMY

In Chapter Four, we reviewed the literature on the economic effect of regulations, particularly of environmental regulations. Here, we add to this, some insights from our dataset to reinforce the ambiguity of the economic impacts of regulation. For our independent variables, we use two constructs: the annual number of economic regulations and the number of environmental regulations in a calendar year. The explanation for what constitutes an economic regulation is in Chapter Two. The definition of environmental regulations can be found above.

If regulations are "job killers," then at a minimum we should be able to measure these effects directly through business metrics such as annual firm births and firm deaths as well as the unemployment rate. Recent studies described in the previous chapter argue the relationship between environmental regulations and employment is ambiguous. As such, the literature offers us the insight that labor market adjustments are a better way to measure whether a relationship exists between the two factors (Walker 2012). In the region, the manufacturing sector accounts for major employment in terms of the total number of employees: 10.6 percent (IN), 17.5 percent (IN), 13.6 percent (MI), 12.2 percent (MN), and 17.6 percent (WI). It also generates the highest source of annual payroll dollars in each state, with the exception of Illinois and Minnesota, where it ranks second. Given that manufacturing generates such a large economic benefit in each of these states, one could imagine that environmental regulations might have a particularly strong impact on the unemployment rate.

If regulations negatively affect local economies, differences in outputs should be discernible in the Gross State Product (GSP), the level of poverty, as well as median household income and per capita personal household income. We identified these constructs as a way to operationalize some of the broader hypothesized effects that may be influenced by regulations (Jaffe et al. 1995; Porter 1998). Because some household income can be earned in jurisdictions outside a person's state of residence, longitudinal changes in household or personal income may be reflective of changes occurring in a regional economy rather than state-specific variations. Still, we do not believe this is a factor in this region, as the average worker's commute is under twenty-four minutes (with a standard deviation of 2.5 minutes).[14]

As discussed in Chapter Four, the area where we expect to find an impact, particularly on small businesses, which represent the largest number of firms

Table 5.2 Relationship between Rules and Firm Deaths/Births

	Correlation Coefficient			
Variables	Economic Rules	1 Yr. Lag	Environment Rules	1 Yr. Lag
Firm Deaths	–0.31*	–0.33*	–0.58^	–0.61^
Firm Births	–0.03	–0.01	–0.12	–0.10
N	25	20	25	20

*$p<0.05$
^$p<0.10$

doing business in the states,[15] is in the per capita number of firm deaths and births annually. Instead, we see as both the number of economic and environmental rules increase, the number of firm deaths decreases. Just as described in the previous chapter, we did not find statistically significant relationships between rules and firm births as displayed in Table 5.2.

One explanation may be that the economic and environmental regulations serve to change the kinds of employment operating in a state. This would mean, however, that regulations can present both positive opportunities for some firms as well as negative effects for others (Porter and van der Linde 1995). When we look at the individual states in the region, we see varying results. But these are again small group observations, making them less reliable. The best explanation is that the number of economic and environmental regulations plays a small role in a business leader's decision-making processes as compared to other factors.

When it comes to the hypothesized relationship between the number of economic and environmental rules and the level of unemployment, we found no statistically significant relationships (Table 5.3). We also found few statistically significant relationships between our measures of regulatory activity and the level of poverty, GSP, median household income, and personal income present mixed results. Where we found significant relationships, they often move in the opposite direction than hypothesized. As in the previous chapter, this may be due to the fact that states with better economic conditions prefer stronger environmental regulations (Quiroga et al. 2009). Of note, the relationship between GSP and environmental regulations is in the opposite direction of the relationship with all regulations, but the association is weak and not statistically significant. It is possible that there is an interactive effect between GSP and the number of environmental regulations, which is discussed in the literature, such as a strained local economy or the presence of an unskilled workforce (Davis and von Wachter 2011). However, the lack of statistical significance prevents such broad conclusions (see Table 5.3).

When it comes to median household income, the direction of the relationship with environmental regulations is in the direction that critics of regulation

Table 5.3 Relationship between Rules and Unemployment and Other Macroeconomic Variables

| Variables | Correlation Coefficient | | | |
	Economic Rules	1 Yr. Lag	Environment Rules	1 Yr. Lag
Unemployment	−0.03	−0.03	−0.04	−0.01
Poverty Level	0.08	0.05	0.11	0.19
GSP	0.29*	0.28^	−0.07	−0.06
Median Household Income	−0.10	−0.11	−0.36*	−0.47*
Personal Household Income	0.19	0.22	−0.24^	−0.21
N	35	30	35	30

*$p<0.05$
^$p<0.10$

hypothesize. In fact, this is the strongest relationship we observed and it is statistically significant at the 0.05 level. Perhaps median income is a more reliable instrument to measure negative economic impacts hypothesized to be correlated to environmental regulations. Walker (2012) points out several problems with using the unemployment rate. First, the unemployment rate only measures those in the labor force who are actively seeking work in the prior four-week period and are currently available for work. The unemployment rate does not distinguish between the unemployed who are collecting benefits and those who are still jobless but have exhausted their benefits. While the labor metric may be a good way to measure individual firm data, median household income may predict changes that are occurring sooner simply because it captures lost wages on a continuous downward slope during unemployment. Second, it is possible that our unemployment data during this period is skewed due to a rare national policy initiative to extend benefits up to 90 months given the chronic and historic unemployment levels following the Great Recession.[16]

Of course it is also possible that median household income is problematic, as it is the only economic indicator that moves significantly in the predicted direction and it did not move in that direction in the cross-sectional analysis undertaken in the previous chapter. We caution against over-interpreting this result.

Overall, the longitudinal findings in the Midwestern region support the cross-sectional analysis for twenty-eight states during 2007 in the previous chapter. Our findings likewise do little to clear up the ambiguity that exists in the literature. Still, this analysis does raise questions about whether the economic constructs are not operationalized in a way that adequately captures the effect of regulation on businesses, whether the appropriate controls are applied, and if the number of regulations has a cumulative influence when accompanied by other economic factors.

In response to our own questions, we believe the variables used in this study and others to measure regulatory burden and economic burden are reliable. The constructs are informed by theory and have been used widely to measure economic outputs; providing both construct and criterion validity. Therefore, we are left to consider another option: Is the effect associated with regulations so small that it is intangible or simply dwarfed by larger factors?

While the effect of regulation is widely acknowledged as hard to isolate among the economic factors that might be influencing business decisions—from customer demand and labor costs to taxation policies—we have a sense that *many* influences matter more than the number of regulations. Empirically, we also know the effects of the Great Recession have had profound effects on businesses.

If "full employment" is assumed to be 4 percent unemployment or less, it is important to note that the region did not enter the Great Recession in great shape. In fact, Michigan was decidedly worse off than its neighbors, while Minnesota's economy was in the best shape. If regulations have a more serious impact during bad economic times (Davis and von Wachter 2011), this may explain some of the stronger correlations we observed in Michigan as they relate to firm births and deaths. Michigan was the only state where there was a negative and statistically significant relationship between environmental regulations and unemployment as well as firm births. Before one takes this conclusion too far, however, Michigan had a positive and statistically significant relationship between all economic regulation and unemployment as well as firm births as observed in Figure 5.4.

However, this may also help explain some of the intensity of the anti-regulation rhetoric during the most recent gubernatorial campaigns in these states, particularly in Michigan. To parse this out farther, we took a look at

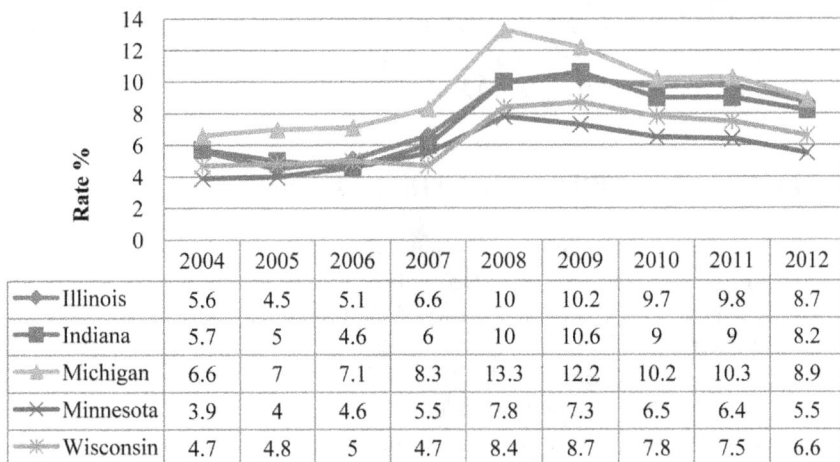

	2004	2005	2006	2007	2008	2009	2010	2011	2012
Illinois	5.6	4.5	5.1	6.6	10	10.2	9.7	9.8	8.7
Indiana	5.7	5	4.6	6	10	10.6	9	9	8.2
Michigan	6.6	7	7.1	8.3	13.3	12.2	10.2	10.3	8.9
Minnesota	3.9	4	4.6	5.5	7.8	7.3	6.5	6.4	5.5
Wisconsin	4.7	4.8	5	4.7	8.4	8.7	7.8	7.5	6.6

Figure 5.4 Regional Unemployment Rate (2004–2012)

the relationship between the number of regulations adopted just prior to the Great Recession (2008) through the end of the study period and the level of unemployment. We wanted to see if the relationship between environmental regulation and unemployment changed during the worst economic conditions in seventy years.

What we found gives very qualified support to the contentions of those who argue that environmental regulations have effects that can intensify when fused with other economic pressures. When we first looked at the impact of rules on the level of unemployment during the study period, we found no significant relationships. However, when we look at the correlation during the recession and the period immediately leading up to it, we see a moderate relationship between environmental rules and unemployment (0.348) that is statistically significant but only at the .10 level of confidence (the relationship for economic regulations is not statistically significant). This lower degree of confidence is likely due to the small number of environmental rules (n =20), which makes the observation less reliable; however, it invites further exploration. Environmental regulations did not have a significant effect on the level of unemployment prior to 2008.

These limited observations (that environmental regulations may have an impact during tougher economic times and that median household income is negatively correlated with environmental regulations) do not change the general observation from this and many other analyses. Keep in mind that all of the other relationships tested (firm births, firm deaths, etc.) showed no relationship. As we stated at the outset, there is little empirical evidence to support the notion that economies and businesses are negatively affected by the total number of regulations in a state. If this is the case (or even if one type of regulation has negative effects during a set of economic conditions that appear twice per century), the question arises as to why it is important for policy-makers to attempt to control the numbers of regulations. To answer this quandary, we must shift our attention to the perception that the number of regulations are purported to have within the regulated community. For this analysis, we surveyed business leaders in the region.

5.5 IN THE EYES OF THE BEHOLDER: BUSINESS EXECUTIVES

While the impact of regulation on an overall state economy is ambiguous and likely minimal, the perceptions held by businesses about the role of regulations are very different than the reality. We conducted a random probability survey in the region during the period of January 2013 through May 2013. More than half of all business leaders in our Midwest region (53 percent) thought the number of regulations has contributed to the economic slow-down over the past five years in the United States. While 30 percent of our respondents believed regulations have been a minor factor, only 10 percent believed they *were not* a factor and the remainder (7 percent) were unsure.

Nearly two-thirds (65 percent) of leaders surveyed in Indiana blame regulatory volume as being a major contributory factor in the country's recent economic slowdown. This is consistent with the earlier reported assessment that 62 percent of Indiana business owners believe that reducing the number of regulations spurs job creation.

National results from a randomly conducted survey of small-business owners (having less than $20 million in sales or revenues) in late October 2011, found similar results.[17] In the poll, conducted by Gallup, small-business owners were asked what they needed most in order for their businesses to thrive in 2012. Fifteen percent said growth in sales, 14 percent said job creation, while 12 percent said fewer government regulations. These findings parallel those we also saw when we asked business executives (in all size firms) which areas of concern were important to their businesses *right now* (see Table 5.6). Because our empirical findings do not reveal a strong correlation between the number of regulations, whether economic or environmental in nature, with economic and business outputs, we hypothesize that *perception* rather than *reality* is influencing the political demand for the reforms ostensibly targeted at controlling this burden.

We are also guided by national polling conducted in the last decade that suggests small businesses perceive that regulations have an impact on their operations. At the same time, survey data also indicate that businesses overall have other priorities; although regulations are important, the prioritization given to them by stakeholders tends to fluctuate as compared to other factors over time. The rising and falling importance of regulation was echoed by business leaders we interviewed in other states.

Participants in our survey were randomly selected from a sample frame of for-profit and non-profit firms[18] operating in the region, of which nine out of ten businesses were for-profit entities. The survey was administered in mixed modes: email invitations were first sent to businesses to participate online. The initial poll contained thirty-one closed-ended questions and five state-specific questions. Of the total, five questions were open-ended. Expecting that the survey length may lower response rates, the fourth and fifth contact attempts utilized a version of the instrument that reduced the state-specific and open-ended questions. About half of the sample completed the longer version. Telephone and facsimile surveys were targeted to those in the sample frame without email; these modes utilized the shorter version of the instrument.

The sample was stratified by state and then by North American Industry Classification System (NAICS) code to ensure a representative sample of industries by state. The sample was weighted by state to ensure it was representative of the proportion of business establishments operating in each state. The sampling error for respondents is + 4.9 percent, at a 95 percent confidence interval. Sample error does not take into account other sources of variation inherent in public opinion studies, such as coverage nonresponse, question wording, or question placement context effects. The verbatim wording of all questions can be found in the Survey Instrument included in the Appendix, along with a full description of the methodology. With the exception of the experimental question and those with ordinal values, the response categories were all randomized.

Given the potential context effects associated with the concept of regulatory burden within the business community, we employed a list-experiment technique in our survey design. Before we asked about regulations and their impact on businesses, we included a list-type question in order to avoid measurement errors that arise when asking about politically infused issues that may introduce bias. No doubt the term "government regulation" has become so infused in our political rhetoric that the mere mention of the concept is likely to conjure up both positive and negative mental images.

The list experiment randomly assigned the sample respondents to one of two groups. Both groups were asked to identify how many proposals recently being talked about they "strongly agree" would "help businesses grow and improve the economy." In the list, we included the following items in this order:

- Eliminating incentives for employers to move jobs overseas
- Increasing consumer purchasing power
- Improving infrastructure like roads, bridges, and water systems
- Making more credit available for businesses
- Reducing the number of regulations

The control group was not asked about "reducing the number of regulations," but the treatment group was provided with the list of *all* proposals. Respondents only received one version of the question (Mutz 2011).

Conceptually, what we get is a value from zero to four for the control group and zero to five for the treatment group. The only difference between the two questions is the addition of the target item (#5) for the treatment group. The analysis consists simply of comparing the *mean* number of items that will "help businesses grow and improve the economy" between the two groups. Because the difference is the presence of the target item, the difference in means represents the share of the sample who "strongly agree" that "reducing the number of regulations" is important for helping businesses grow and improve the economy.

Our results follow in Table 5.4.

The difference between these two means is statistically significant.

Table 5.4 List Experiment to Measure Regulatory Awareness

Question		N	Mean	Std Deviation
Q6A	Control	106	3.23	1.287
Q6B	Target	113	3.80	1.199

Asked at the start of the survey, before question order can affect the context of responses, we see that 56 percent (3.80–3.24) of the sample "strongly agree" that reducing the number of regulations is important to "help businesses grow and improve the economy." Note that this is *not* generalizable to business leaders in the five-state region. This is an experiment, and it is analyzed without using weights to match the sample to the public.[19] The overall lesson from the list experiment is that for a significant number of business executives, the idea of reducing the number of regulations does, in fact, resonate within the business community.

To drill down further, we later asked business leaders to identify those laws and regulations that have had the greatest impact on their operations during the past five years. When asking detailed questions on topics with low salience, methodologically we know we risk increasing nonresponse error (Dillman et al. 2009). In fact, for those respondents who completed the survey online, just one-third completed the state specific questions. This may be a reflection of response fatigue that is associated with questionnaire length or item nonresponse that results when asking about issues that are not easily recalled (Dillman et al. 2009).

To make this task easier, we selected comprehensive environmental laws from those measures adopted within the last two years and environmental regulations adopted during the period of study. Overall, we found respondents were unfamiliar with these new laws passed in their states. Although aiding recall, this close-ended option approach, which excluded less recent enactments as well as regulations on the books for more than a decade, arguably may have served to omit some measures with significant implications for businesses. To counter this effect, we first offered respondents the opportunity to tell us in an open-ended question which law or regulation has had the greatest impact on their business operations.[20] Table 5.5 summarizes what we found.

In almost every state, just one in ten business executives identified a specific law or regulation having the most impact on their business operations in recent years. In only a few instances did respondents provide us with an example of a state-specific law or regulation. More than half of the coded responses reported federal laws or regulations. Across the board, references

Table 5.5 Percentage of Respondents Identifying *No* Specific Laws or Regulations

State	Environmental Laws	Environmental Regulations
Illinois	89%	91%
Indiana	86%	87%
Michigan	90%	93%
Minnesota	95%	96%
Wisconsin	92%	94%

were made to federal measures including "Obamacare," OSHA and SBA requirements, as well as the municipal permitting requirements governing hazardous waste removal.

These findings support the idea that regulatory burden is a *perceived* problem among the business community given the absence of readily identifiable examples.[21] Recall too, that when we asked business leaders about their views at the start of the survey, 53 percent thought the number of regulations has contributed to the economic slowdown over the past five years. Yet, we also want to point out that the timing of the survey may have heightened this perception. Our own hypothesis embraces the notion that negative perceptions among business leaders about regulations may be more pronounced when the overall economy is strained. This survey was fielded during a period when business leaders' recent memories of the business climate were dismal, and the future did not look overly optimistic. When we first asked respondents how they would rate their state's business climate over the past five years, only 2 percent said "excellent" and 23 percent said "good." Almost three-quarter of all respondents (74 percent) said the business climate in their state was "fair to poor."

As far as the future is concerned, the picture was a bit more optimistic—but not for everyone. Forty-five percent of business executives think their state's business climate will get "better" over the next five years, 22 percent think it will get "worse," 26 percent think it will stay the same, and 7 percent are unsure.[22] In terms of predicting future expectations, party affiliation is one of the most significant determinants. Fifty-one percent of Democrats think their state's business climate will get "better" as compared to 48 percent of Independents and only 36 percent of all Republicans. This sheds more light on the overall quandary facing elected officials—and those who aspire to be elected in the future. Republican business leaders are much more pessimistic about the future. And now comes the really bad news for some politicians; 40 percent of the business executives we randomly surveyed are Republicans as compared to just 16 percent who were Democrats.[22]

We then asked business leaders—of which 40 percent were the chief executive or financial officer in their company and 40 percent were the owner or partner in the firm—to tell us which areas of concerns were important to their businesses *right then*. Respondents were queried about a range of issues including those regularly surveyed in national polling in the past. Among those who "strongly agreed," 61 percent said it is the cost of employee health benefits and 56 percent said the number of government regulations. A similar proportion (55 percent) said it is the amount of taxes paid by their business. These responses (along with complying with regulations and the uncertainty associated with regulations) were significantly greater than the other measures in terms of strength of agreement displayed in Table 5.6.

Respondents were not limited in the number of business concerns they could identify, so we also asked them to select the *most* important concern

Table 5.6 Important Area of Concern for Your Business *Right Now*

	Employee Health Care Benefits	Number of Gov't Regulations	Business Taxes Paid	Uncertainty of Futyre Regulations	Complying with Regulations	Skilled Workers	Weak Demand	Available Credit
Strongly Agree	61%	56%	55%	50%	48%	32%	33%	25%
Somewhat Agree	18%	19%	25%	26%	31%	35%	34%	29%
Somewhat Disagree	4%	11%	9%	9%	10%	18%	17%	22%
Strongly Disagree	9%	11%	9%	7%	9%	5%	13%	17%
Don't Know	8%	3%	3%	7%	3%	2%	2%	7%

Table 5.7 Ranked Business Concerns

Cost of employee health benefits	22%
Amount of business taxes paid	16%
Number of government regulations	13%
Weak customer demand	13%
Complying with government regulations	12%
Lack of credit opportunity	9%
Uncertainty about future regulations	8%
Quality and skills of workers	6%

among all those they selected. Here we gain some insight into the priorities set by businesses. When ranked from highest to lowest, we see that direct cost expenditures—employee health care benefits and business taxes—top the lists of those concerns *most* important to businesses. Still, the number of regulations ranks third as the most important concern today. Table 5.7 summarizes these findings.

Since regulations ranked high among those concerns we attempted to identify the specific kinds of regulations that evoked the most concern for those in the regulated community. We asked respondents about the kind of regulations having the most significant impact on their state's economy. Table 5.8 shows a ranking of those regulations posing the biggest problems.

Here again, the number of regulations is among the top concern for business leaders.

A focus on regulatory burden also ranked high in terms of the priority business executives believe their political leaders should set. Compared to other business priorities in their state, 48 percent of respondents said reducing the number of regulations should be a high priority for their state legislature and governor. Another third (34 percent) said it should be a medium priority, and only 15 percent said it should be a low priority. As expected, we found a moderate and statistically significant relationship between the need for government leaders to prioritize reducing the number regulations

Table 5.8 Top Ranked Business Concerns

Employee benefit regulations	76%
Number of government regulations	75%
Fee generating regulations	56%
Environmental compliance regulations	55%
Licensing regulations	53%
Civil fines	46%
Other regulations	8%

in their state and beliefs about how government regulations have affected a state's business climate.

We also looked at whether the perception of the impact government regulations are having on a state's business climate influences perceptions on how governmental priorities should be set. We found that 72 percent of those who believed government regulations have made the state's business climate worse believed the legislature and governor should prioritize reducing the number of government regulations. Only two respondents who believed the business climate has been made better by government regulations believe that reducing regulations should be a high priority for policy-makers. The chi-square statistic was significant ($p=.000$), meaning we can reject the null hypothesis that executives' assessments about government regulations do not influence their evaluations of how policy-makers should set priorities.

We find an even stronger relationship between the impact regulations have had on the economic slowdown in the United States, and the setting of policy priorities in the states. The relationship between these two factors is very strong (0.673) and statistically significant at the 5 percent level. Seventy-eight percent of those who believed the number of regulations have contributed to the economic slowdown over the past five years in the United States believed reducing the number of regulations should be a high priority for their state's legislature and governor. Comparatively, six out of ten of those who thought regulations have only been a minor factor in the economic slowdown thought reducing the number of regulations should be a medium priority in their state capital compared to 20 percent of those who thought the number of regulations has played a major role in the economic slowdown.

Interestingly, there was a widely held belief that not all regulations are bad regulations. We found this sentiment shared by the business leaders we surveyed. More than nine out of ten of all business executives generally agreed that some form of regulation of business is necessary for a modern economy. Almost everyone agreed (96 percent) that they could live with "regulation if it is fair, manageable, and reasonable." Among these business leaders, 61 percent "strongly agreed" they can live with some degree of fair regulations. Only 8 percent believed we should "get rid of all government regulation on businesses."

Two factors appear to contribute strongly to the current perceptions about the impact of regulations in the region today. The state of the economy, at least for now, appears to be driving perceptions about regulatory burden in the region among the business executives we surveyed. Party affiliation also divides the perspectives of business leaders on almost every measurement we surveyed. Consider the following chasms:

- Sixty-three percent of Republicans thought the number of regulations has been a major contributing factor in the economic slowdown as compared to 26 percent of Democrats and 50 percent of Independents.

- Sixty-seven percent of Republicans believed the number of regulations should be a priority for the governor and legislature as compared to 23 percent of Democrats and 42 percent of Independents.
- Additionally, 73 percent of Republicans strongly agreed that the number of regulations is an important area of concern right now for their businesses as compared to 22 percent of Democrats and 50 percent of Independents.

These findings are critical to understanding the motivations for politicians in enacting regulatory reforms. In dealing with regulations, politicians face a peculiar problem:

- First, the volume of regulation is perceived by business leaders to hurt their economic prospects.
- But the evidence that it really hurts their prospects is limited.
- There are few particular regulations that business leaders can identify as causing problems. Furthermore, the laws in which regulations find their origin are popular and even business owners largely recognize the need for regulation.[23]
- Finally, party ideology is a strong indicator of what factors shape the perspectives of business leaders.

Are regulatory reforms the way of squaring this circle? They allow politicians to be responsive to the concern about regulation but at the same time not undermine the goals regulation is designed to achieve.

This argument needs further exploration. In the next two chapters, we turn to the question of motivations for politicians enacting regulatory reform. First through an aggregate analysis and then with two case studies in which we attempt to understand why politicians turn to a policy approach of limited effectiveness. While we do find that other motivations play a role, we come back to the findings of this survey. Regulatory reform is attractive to politicians because it is a low-cost way of addressing the perceived problem of the number of regulations.

6 Alternative Explanations for Regulatory Reform

Regulatory reforms appear to have little effect on the number of regulations. Politicians, particularly those in legislatures, appear to have influence over regulatory policy by voting yea or no on regulatory statutes (and perhaps through the budgetary process and the appointment process (Wood and Waterman 1991)) and do not need procedural controls to exert this influence. If regulatory reforms are not critical to regulatory decision-making, then why are they enacted? A first thought is that regulations have such a large impact on society that even small, impossible to measure effects are enough to justify the use of regulatory reforms to influence them.

But that does not appear to be the case. The literature on the relationship between regulations and the economy finds minimal impacts. This is supported by the literature review in Chapter Four, where no consistent relationship between regulation and economic indicators was found. Similarly, in most of the analyses of the five Midwestern states in Chapter Five, differences in the volume of regulations overall, and environmental regulations in particular, appeared to have little effect on macroeconomic variables over a seven-year period.

Interestingly, our survey of Midwestern business owners points out one possible answer. Business owners believe that the number of regulations is a problem for them. They may believe this because of the rhetoric from politicians condemning regulations, which has shown a marked increase since the onset of the Great Recession (Livermore et al. 2012). Or they may believe it because of an overall sense that their autonomy to make decisions has been impeded by the sheer combined volume of federal, state, and local regulations. Whether or not it is caused by political bombast, this perception is a problem for politicians, even the ones who use the rhetoric. With voters (and possible campaign donors) demanding that something be done about regulations, politicians are under pressure to do something. This still raises the question of why regulatory reform is seen as the answer to the problem, since it is a tool that seems to do little to reduce the volume of regulation. Why not repeal regulations or change the organic statutes that authorize agencies to issue regulations? After all, the analysis in Chapter Five shows that a source of regulation is laws passed by these same legislators.

In this chapter we examine other possible motivations. Some are consistent with earlier hypotheses; others are more grounded in theories of political decision-making at the state level than in theories of regulation. One theory is the idea that legislatures and governors are in competition for policy influence and that regulatory reform is one front in this battle. Another theory is that the political culture of a state has a profound influence on policy decisions. Yet another is that varying degrees of legislative professionalism lead state legislators to make different decisions. Finally, we examine the policy diffusion argument that states are influenced by their neighbors when adopting innovative policies.

These explanations provide some additional insights but little that is dispositive. With the theories of regulation failing to provide a comprehensive explanation for regulatory reform, and the failure of some of these alternative explanations, we return to the explanations of legislative behavior rather than theories of regulation. The particular arguments of Mayhew (2004) and Fiorina (1989), that politicians engage in "position taking" and "credit claiming," begin to look like a more attractive explanation as other hypotheses fail. They also gain support from the perceptions about regulation discovered in the survey of Midwestern business owners. In the next chapter, we look at two states with among the most complicated regulatory procedural environments and examine these theories in more detail.

This chapter proceeds as follows. The first section is a cataloging of other work on the motivations of state policy-makers. The findings of these works point us toward other explanations for regulatory reforms. In Section 6.2, we describe our data to test these explanations and present correlations and simple regressions for explanations of regulatory reform. Section 6.3 is a discussion of the implications of these findings. In Section 6.4, we summarize what we have learned about the motivation for regulatory reform to date, reopening the possibility that regulatory reform is merely an attempt to get credit for addressing a problem that may not exist.

6.1 SO WHY *ELSE* MIGHT AGENCIES ENACT REGULATORY REFORMS?

Applying the theories of the regulatory state found in Chapter One to regulatory reforms is largely predicated upon regulatory reforms actually working. If regulatory reforms are means by which powerful interests can control regulatory decisions, then we would expect to see some evidence of regulatory decisions changing as a result of regulatory reforms. Similarly, if regulatory reforms made regulatory decisions more democratic, more prone to interest group competition, amenable to political control, or insulated experts from influence then again we would expect decisions to somehow vary with the extent of regulatory reform.

However, if, as concluded in Chapters Two and Three, regulatory reforms are not effective in affecting the number of regulations (and therefore unlikely to be effective in changing the content of regulations), it leaves open the question of why their presence has exploded in states over the past decade? To answer this question, we turn to literature on the motivations of state legislators (and governors). Some of this literature is particular to the regulatory arena, but we also consider sources from other policy areas in developing hypotheses for the motivation for regulatory reforms.

Rossi (2001) called for greater study of the origin of differences in state regulatory processes a decade ago, emphasizing the need for more examination of the variations in state Administrative Procedure Acts. Some of the best work in this area, however, is more than two decades old. Clingermayer and West (1992) tried to explain why certain states adopt certain procedures but found few discernible patterns. Their conclusion mirrors some of what we have found here, that "the lack of robustness in some of the models examined here suggests the possibility that no theoretical argument that we have developed thus far truly accounts for these administrative institutions" (53).

Party Affiliation of Officeholders

Several works examine the role of political ideology in preferences for regulatory reforms. Grady and Simon (2002), who developed a scale for the extent of legislative control of agency rulemaking, argue that party affiliation explains much of the preference for regulatory oversight:

> The most important relationship was between Republican gains in state legislatures and increased control over rule making either by citizen access or institutional control. In the 1994 election cycle, Republican candidates promised to reduce the role of government, and they attempted to achieve that pledge through restricting administrative autonomy, at least during rule making. For every method of measuring the effect of partisanship, this result was obtained. (671)

Similarly, much of the nonacademic literature criticizing regulatory reforms as attempts to hobble agency decision-making is written by supporters of regulation who argue that reforms are deliberate attempts to stall or stop regulatory initiatives (Vladeck and McGarity 1995). For that reason, the first independent variables we tested as possible causal factors for the decision to enact regulatory reform were party control of the governor's mansion and the legislature.

There is also an argument that control of the bureaucracy is more appealing in times of divided government. In the welfare policy context, Volden (2002) casts doubt on this assertion in an empirical study showing that the propensity to delegate decisions to agencies does not vary with the presence of divided government. Since regulatory reforms are long-term structural mechanisms, it makes sense that a short-term condition such as divided government is unlikely to motivate political actors to implement them. If, however, divided government is the norm in a state, a legislature might be more likely to put controls on executive branch behavior. And the executive branch may be more likely to desire influence over agency decisions at the expense of the legislature.

Gubernatorial and Legislative Power

The comparative power of governors and legislatures varies considerably across the states. Numerous scholars have measured the power of governors (Beyle 1995) and legislatures (Jewell and Whicker 1994). In states such as New Jersey, the governor is widely perceived as powerful because (s)he is the only state official elected statewide (save for a lieutenant governor who runs on a ticket with the governor). In other states such as Texas, the legislature is seen to be the primary policy-making body.

To be clear, this is a separate measure of institutional power than the dependent variables constructed from the extent of legislative and executive regulatory review in the states. Those variables measure the stringency of legislative and executive review of regulations. The power variables are intended to capture the extent of the *other* powers of the governor and legislature. These powers could vary from appointment power, budgetary control, the presence of term limits, and other oversight powers. A governor who already has strong control over the executive branch, may be less likely to seek strong regulatory review powers. Nonetheless, strong gubernatorial power may prompt legislatures to enact regulatory reforms to constrain the governor. The inverse would likely be true for legislative power. All of this is further influenced by how party competition; party control between the chambers as well as the governorship affects the internal processes of governing (Rosenthal et al. 2002). Monolithic control over the legislative chambers and the executive branch is unlikely to prompt calls for regulatory control.

Legislative Professionalism

Unlike in the federal government, where Congress is populated by individuals who work full time at their legislative duties, there is considerable variation in the makeup of state legislatures. Given the diverse structures in legislatures across the fifty states, professionalism has and continues to be used to distinguish those bodies that more closely mirror the inner workings of Congress in terms of resources and legislative scope from the citizen legislatures, which meet less frequently and are vested with fewer resources (Squire 1988, 1992). Professionalism has also been used to measure causal effects on diversity, divided governments, and legislative form and function (Squire 1992).

Squire (1992) argues that more professional legislatures do what is best to promote their members' interests. If legislators perceive that regulatory reform is in their interests (either because it will help them control regulatory decisions or because they can use it to get credit for responding to concerns about regulation), then we might expect that more professional legislatures are more likely to enact regulatory reform measures. A consistent measurement of professionalism in the state legislatures includes an index of members' pay, staff members per legislator, and total days in session.

Political Culture

The ideology of a state's citizenry may also make a difference in the adoption of regulatory reforms. While we tested party control of the branches of government as described above, these are an imperfect measure of the ideology of the citizens (Berry et al. 1998). A Democrat in Massachusetts is different than a Democrat in Wyoming. While this variable is likely to be somewhat colinear with party control (particularly as Republicans made electoral gains in the south throughout the 2000s), we tested each measure of ideology.

Adoption in Nearby States

Walker (1969) conducted an important study on the factors that lead to innovative policies in the states. The factor that he found most critical was that adoption of similar policies in nearby states. He notes:

> In all cases, however, the likelihood of a state adopting a new program is higher if other states have already adopted the idea. The likelihood becomes higher still if the innovation has been adopted by a state viewed by key decision makers as a point of legitimate comparison. Decision makers are likely to adopt new programs, therefore, when they become convinced that their state is relatively deprived, or that some need exists to which other states in their "league" have already responded. (897)

Gray (1973), however, found some difficulties with Walker's analysis. She felt that Walker grouped policy areas together, and that by decoupling policy areas, diffusion patterns differed and other factors appeared to influence adoption of innovative policies.

The study of diffusion of policies has become much more nuanced in the decades since Walker and Gray. Of particular interest, Shipan and Volden (2008) argue that one reason for diffusion is economic competition between states. If one state adopts a policy to make it more attractive to firms deciding where to locate, nearby states may do so as well so as to not lose firms to the original adopter. Regulatory reforms certainly qualify as innovations that may appear to improve the economic climate. Therefore, the inclusion of a measure of adoption of a particular reform in nearby states should be included as a possible explanatory variable for adoption in the state in question.

6.2 DATA AND ANALYSIS

To analyze these "other factors" that may influence state adoption of regulatory reform, we draw on the Institute for Policy Integrity (IPI) assessment of regulatory reforms in the states. As readers will recall, we gave each of the twenty-eight states analyzed in Chapter Two a zero-ten-point score for the stringency of three of their regulatory procedures—gubernatorial review, legislative review, and economic analysis—based on the IPI data. For this chapter, we scored the additional twenty-two states based on the data in the IPI report. These three variables become our dependent variable for the analysis below.[1]

We then operationalized the independent variables discussed in the previous section. Many of these variables have a significant literature backing their construction. Because regulatory reforms are not adopted at identical points in time, when creating some of these variables we had to make decisions regarding their timing. For example, party control of the governor's office and the state legislature varied over the course of the 2000s, the decade when the pace of regulatory reform quickened. In this case we created a variable based on control in 2004, 2006, and 2008. If Democrats controlled the governor's office (or the legislature) in each of these years, the variable was given a value of "3," in two of these years a "2," etc. If control of the legislature was split between the parties, then the value for that year was 0.5 (giving the legislative control variable possible values of 0, 0.5, 1, 1.5, 2, 2.5, or 3). In the analysis below, we looked at both the overall variation of regulatory reform with party control, and what happened in those states when control did or did not change.

For divided government, we examined the same three years: 2004, 2006, and 2008. A dummy variable was created if the state experienced divided government in any of the three years counted. Thirty-six of the fifty states had at least one period of divided government during the study period. We also looked at behavior in states where divided government persisted through all three study years.

For legislative professionalism, we adopted Squire's measure of professionalism. Using the U.S. Congress as a baseline, Squire (1992) used the time in session, salary, and staffing levels to create a continuous variable (with a 0 to 1 scale) for state legislative professionalism. The most frequently used scale for legislative power was developed by Jewell and Whicker (1994). While the power index they envisioned looked at institutional and leadership powers, we focused our attention on just the former. Based on their construct measuring institutional powers, we devised a six-point scale. The scale gave a higher score when there were no limits on the length of a legislative session, when there is no public initiative process, and when the governor does not have a line item veto. We used the 2001 values for the variable (they do not vary much over time).

For gubernatorial power, Thad Beyle developed a gubernatorial institutional power score in 1960; the indices are adjusted regularly.[2] Beyle's index captures six attributes to gauge a Governor's Institutional Power Score (GIP), which he distinguishes from a Governor's Personal Power Index Score (GPP). For this analysis, states ranked with a higher GIP indicate higher gubernatorial institutional strength. The six components of GIP include gubernatorial tenure potential, appointment power, budget power, veto power, and party control as well as the number of separately elected statewide policy officials. We used the 2005 values for this variable, and like the legislative strength variable, they do not vary much over time.

As described above, we wanted to include an ideology variable in addition to a variable for party control in our analysis. Berry et al. (1998) developed a scale for citizen ideology that is based on the voting records of the members of the states' congressional delegations. They have updated their values through 2010,[3] and for our analysis we averaged the values for the states from 2001 to 2010 since regulatory reforms were enacted throughout the decade.

To measure diffusion effects, we averaged the scores for each of the dependent variables in the states that bordered each state. For example, a "presence in nearby states" variable for gubernatorial review for Maine would consist of the average of the gubernatorial review scores for Massachusetts and New Hampshire. Similar analysis was conducted for legislative review and economic analysis variables.

Table 6.1 below shows the correlation coefficients for each of our independent variables (including state population) with our three dependent variables (the extent of state gubernatorial regulatory oversight, legislative oversight, and analytical requirements).

Next we ran ordinary least squares regressions on each of the three dependent variables. We assumed a simple linear relationship between the three dependent variables and the independent variables. The results are presented below in Tables 6.2–6.4.

None of the party, institutional powers, or governance variables had a statistically significant relationship with executive review of regulations at the 5 percent level. Although this regression represents the final nested model, there was not much change as the variables were added to the model and each did little to increase the variation in the dependent variable. Also, the F statistic ($p < 0.09$) indicates that we cannot reject the null that all of the coefficients of our independent variables are equal to zero.

Next, we looked at the influence party, institutional powers, and governance had on legislative review in Table 6.3. Here again, we report the final nested model as there was very little variance in the earlier models.

Table 6.1 Correlations among Institutional Review and Political Factors

	Executive Review	Legislative Review	Fiscal Analysis
Party of Governor (1 = Democrat)	−0.05	0.07	0.09
Party Control of Legislature (More Democratic Is Higher)	−0.09	−0.07	−0.07
Likelihood of Divided Government	0.21^	−0.1	0.17
Citizen Ideology (More Liberal Is Higher)	0.05	−0.27**	0.01
Population	0.04	−0.19	0.29**
Legislative Professionalism	0.33**	−0.29**	0.34**
Presence in Nearby State	0.14	−0.04	0.04
Power of the Governor	0.09	0.06	0.09
Power of the Legislature	−.3**	−0.02	−0.09

^ Significant at 10% level
** Significant at 5% level

Also the F statistic ($p < 0.51$), indicates that we cannot reject the null that all of the coefficients of our independent variables are equal to zero. However, we do find a statistically significant relationship ($p < 0.053$) between legislative professionalism and legislative review, but it moves in

Table 6.2 Estimated Coefficients for the Executive Review Model

Estimated final model from a nested OLS model of executive review (10 pt. scale) by gubernatorial party, legislative party, gubernatorial and legislative power, divided government, and legislative professionalism in 50 states (2010 data).

Final Model Party, Institutional Powers, and Governance		
Variable	Coeff.	s.e.
Intercept	−6.05	6.40
Gubernatorial Party	−0.42	0.44
Legislative Party	−0.64	0.46
Gubernatorial Power	1.87	1.67
Legislative Power	0.79	0.54
Divided Government	2.44	1.43
Legislative Professionalism^	7.60	4.14
F-Statistic (df)	1.99 (6)	
Adjusted R^2	0.1099	

$p < 0.05$*
$p < 0.10$^

Table 6.3 Estimated Coefficients for the Legislative Review Model

Estimated final model from a nested OLS model of legislative review (10 pt. scale) by gubernatorial party, legislative party, gubernatorial and legislative power, divided government, and legislative professionalism in 50 states (2010 data).

	Final Model Party, Institutional Powers, and Governance	
Variable	Coeff.	s.e.
Intercept	3.14	5.07
Gubernatorial Party	–.088	0.37
Legislative Party	–0.64	0.46
Gubernatorial Power	0.95	1.36
Legislative Power	0.01	0.31
Divided Government	–0.05	1.17
Legislative Professionalism*	–6.86	3.44
F-Statistic (df)	0.89 (6)	
Adjusted R^2	–0.014	

$p < 0.05$*

a direction other than hypothesized. We expected to find more professional legislatures with more legislative review mechanism in place. But it may be that professional legislatures have other powers at their disposal to oversee the regulatory regime such as stronger budget authorities and more staff resources. Conversely, citizen legislatures with fewer resources also spend less time in their state capitals, so there are fewer opportunities to oversee bureaucracies. This may explain why less professional legislatures appear to have more mandatory regulatory review techniques in place. Explaining the genesis for the independent review commission that exists in Pennsylvania, one oversight commissioner characterized it this way:

> There had been, for several years, a growing feeling within the legislature, House and Senate, that agencies were creating their own policy through the regulatory process; that they were taking statutes the legislature would pass, and issuing regulations which at times the legislature felt were contrary to legislative intent . . . and those regulations were having an impact on the regulated communities, on economic development in Pennsylvania, on businesses in Pennsylvania, and consumers in Pennsylvania. So this [Independent Regulatory Review Commission, IRRC] was a means to [address the problem]. The legislature I assume was wise enough to realize their plight. They had enough on their plate and they couldn't review every single regulation. But they could assign committees with oversight and more importantly you could develop an independent commission to do the actual in

depth research and apply whatever criteria the legislature ended up putting into the IRRC law.

Lastly, we modeled the influence party, institutional powers, and governance have on the degree of economic analysis taking place in states (see Table 6.4).

Again, the overall fit of the model is poor as reported by the adjusted R^2 statistic, and we cannot be sure that all the coefficients are not equal to zero as determined by the F statistic ($p < 0.147$). Legislative professionalism is statistically significant at the $p < 0.1$ level.

The results on the surface are discouraging. The only variable that is consistently significant is legislative professionalism. Legislative professionalism is positively correlated with executive review and regulatory analysis and negatively correlated with legislative review. A few other variables have significant correlations with the dependent variables but lose their significance when other variables are controlled for in the regressions.[4]

However, the fact that legislative professionalism is significant and that other variables such as divided government and the power of the legislature are significant in some limited circumstances is instructive. Coupled with the fact that party control, ideology, and policy diffusion appear to have little effect on the presence of regulatory reforms, the variables that are significant point to the idea that the choice to enact regulatory reform may be influenced more by factors internal to state government than by outside conditions. We discuss this further below.

Table 6.4 Estimated Coefficients for the Economic Analysis Model

Estimated final model from a nested OLS model of fiscal analysis (10 pt. scale) by gubernatorial party, legislative party, gubernatorial and legislative power, divided government, and legislative professionalism in 50 states (2010 data).

Variable	Final Model Party, Institutional Powers, and Governance		
	Coeff.		s.e.
Intercept	−3.81		6.28
Gubernatorial Party	−0.34		0.44
Legislative Party	−.057		0.46
Gubernatorial Power	1.42		1.68
Legislative Power	0.79		0.54
Divided Government	2.29		1.45
Legislative Professionalism^	8.06		4.26
F-Statistic (df)		1.69 (6)	
Adjusted R^2		0.079	

$p < 0.05*$
$p < 0.1$^

6.3 DISCUSSION OF RESULTS

In Chapters Two and Three, we reinforced the conclusion about regulatory reforms that is prevalent in the empirical literature. The consequences, both negative and positive, of regulatory procedures added to the regulatory process are limited. Regulatory reform does not lead to a wholesale abandonment (or even a noticeable partial abandonment) of regulation writing by agencies. Nor does it enshrine the will of the enacting coalition by "stacking the deck" faced by agencies when they make regulatory decisions. The impact of regulatory reform appears at most to be occasional and marginal.

However, the enactment of regulatory reforms continues unabated. Many of the theories of the regulatory state argue that regulations and, by extension, regulatory reforms are about the allocation of power between outside interests. But maybe regulations and regulatory reforms are different in this regard. Regulations reallocate resources between different groups of society, often from firms and toward the general public. The discussion in Chapters Four and Five show that this reallocation is not large enough to have macroeconomic impacts, but the results of the survey in Chapter Five show that despite this lack of large-scale impacts, business owners do feel burdened by the volume of regulations. Nonetheless, they are hard pressed to name particular regulations that are a problem.

Legislators and executives, however, have to walk a fine line. Much of the public supports the goals of regulation such as protecting public health and the environment. Even Governor Walker of Wisconsin, who highlighted his administration's effort to eliminate unnecessary regulations in his State of the State address, only did so after setting this precondition: The only measures suitable for repeal or modifications were those regulations whose repeal did not "creat(e) a negative impact on public health or the environment."[5] How does a politician who wants to be responsive to particular constituents with a concern about a regulation do so without eliminating the regulation and angering a still larger number of constituents?

One possibility is that regulatory reforms are popular because they provide the answer to this question. Legislators in particular present themselves as "outsiders" sometimes attacking their own institutions (Rosenthal et al. 2002). It is likely this extends to bureaucracies. Rosenthal et al. (2002) argue that members are often frustrated by the process and their failure to advance their own policy agendas. When this happens, they observe: "Rarely do legislators blame themselves for what they fail to achieve . . . When they succeed, they claim credit; when they fail, and it is the fault of the 'system'"(25). One way to fix a regulatory system problem is with a regulatory reform.

If this is true, the best explanation for regulatory reform may come from work on legislative behavior that predates the large increase in regulatory reforms that began in the late 1970s. Mayhew describes legislators as motivated by reelection, and two of the behaviors they engage in to ensure reelection are "position taking" and "credit claiming." Regulatory reforms are all sold as ways to "fix" regulation. Analytical requirements will lead to less costly regulations. Requirements for enhanced participation will make clueless bureaucrats more responsive to the public (or to a particular public if the requirement is to give a group such as small businesses enhanced standing before agencies). Requirements for executive or legislative review give those complaining about regulation the assurance that we (the governor or the legislature) will be watching over the shoulders of the regulators. All of these have undeniable rhetorical appeal and may assuage the constituency dissatisfied with regulations. If we see legislators as "credit seeking" and "blame avoiding" (Fiorina 1982), regulatory reform fits nicely in this vision.

Fiorina points us toward another possible motivation for regulatory reform. He argued that casework had become an increasingly important part of the job of members of Congress. He examined the increasing advantage of incumbents and, after eliminating a number of hypotheses for this advantage, settled on the growth in constituent service as an explanation. In addition to information gleaned using case studies of specific members of Congress, he cited the growth of home district Congressional staffs as evidence that casework had grown in importance. In work with Noll (Fiorina and Noll 1978b), he developed a theoretical model explaining the motivation for representatives to create bureaucracies and then to devote substantial resources to intervening in the decisions of those bureaucracies.

Fiorina (2008) has since argued that because the public has become accustomed to casework, party ideology has begun to gain in importance again. However, state legislatures are different than Congress. They represent a smaller number of constituents and rely more upon casework and less upon ideology to identify themselves to those who vote in their district (Rosenthal 2004).[6] Fiorina's argument about casework likely still applies to state legislators even if its importance to national legislators has diminished. Rosenthal et al. (2002) note that although there are variances in the states, up to two-thirds of legislators would rank constituent service as the most important aspect of their work.

And regulatory reform provides many ways for legislators (or governors) to intervene on behalf of a constituent on a particular issue. Executive or legislative review allows for direct intervention. Participation requirements allow legislators to file comments with the agency that doubtlessly carry weight beyond those filed by an ordinary citizen (an argument supported by interviews documented in Chapter 7). Even the most technocratic of regulatory reforms, economic analysis, can be seen as a way of forcing agencies to provide political overseers with more information about their regulatory decisions, and therefore more ways to object to those decisions (Whisnant and DeWitt Cherry 1996).

In other words, while the rhetoric of regulatory reform is high-minded and policy oriented, the reality may be fundamentally political. The only variables that showed any significance had to do with the motivations of state legislatures and governors. When enacting and implementing new procedures for the regulatory process, political actors are not helping those who are upset with regulation, but rather they are helping themselves. That is why we see states with higher levels of legislative professionalism more likely to impose analytical requirements that will help them intervene in the occasional regulatory decision and get credit for responding to concerns about regulation (as noted above, Squire (1992) argues that more professional legislatures are more likely to pass measures designed to help their membership).[7]

The finding that legislative professionalism also leads to more stringent executive review argues for a role for interbranch competition for oversight of the regulatory state. Governors confronted with more professional legislatures use executive review to ensure that they have a viable ability to intervene in regulatory decisions should the need arise. Governors do not want interest groups thinking that the legislature is the only branch that they can go to do deal with problems caused by a particular regulation. This is also supported by the mild correlation between divided government and executive review.

Gubernatorial and legislative powers do not show significant relationships with executive and legislative review, respectively. If governors are already powerful due to appointment power or other mechanisms, then executive review becomes a less necessary option for them. Similarly, if legislators are the dominant players in state policy-making, then the decision whether or not to set up a legislative review process rests on other factors.

What the decision to enact regulatory reforms does not appear to be related to is any policy problem or ideological preference related to regulation (party control and citizen ideology were uncorrelated to regulatory reform). And this makes sense, because as we found earlier, regulatory reform measures do not have significant impacts on regulation. Instead, we believe that the most convincing explanation for regulatory reform is that it is a form of credit seeking by politicians eager to appear responsive to concerns about regulation but unwilling to engage in the more politically difficult task of passing more specific laws or repealing agency regulatory decisions.

6.4 THE NEED TO LOOK MORE CLOSELY

We are now closer to solving the mystery of regulatory reform. Many theories of the regulatory state aim to posit a broad explanation of the influences upon agency regulatory decisions. As Wilson (1989) cautioned and Carrigan and Coglianese (2011) echoed however, "Any analysis of a process that can have so many moving political parts and institutional features will undoubtedly make it difficult to derive and sustain empirically broad generalizations" (Carrigan and Coglianese 2011, 113). Indeed, many of our attempts to find categorical explanations for the enactment of regulatory reforms have fallen short.

However, the absence of evidence is also very informative. It suggests that the reasons given for regulatory reform by advocates and by critics should not be taken at face value. The epiphenomenal nature of regulatory reform demonstrated in Chapters Two and Three suggests that it is often a technique used by politicians to appear to be dealing with an issue without really addressing it. If it brings with it the added benefit of allowing political actors to interject themselves into agency decisions and hence to appear to be responsive in the future to constituents as suggested by Fiorina (1989), then all the better.

This is the type of explanation, however, that will never be demonstrable in large-scale empirical studies. Therefore, in the next chapter we examine two states with extensive means for regulatory reform in more detail. James Q. Wilson, one of the most prominent scholars of bureaucracy and regulation, was a proponent of understanding how government worked by actually talking to those who worked there. Chapter Seven is an attempt to do that in two states, and to examine the motivations that legislators, governors, and interest groups possess when they enact and implement regulatory reforms.

7 Regulatory Reform
Rhetoric and Reality in Pennsylvania and North Carolina

> I don't think I ever met a business person who has said that a regulation
> is good for economic development . . . I am not here to say all regula-
> tions are bad . . . some are necessary to address the real problems that
> exist . . . But the reality is every single regulation has a cost and the
> costs keep going up.
>
> Shawn Good, Director of Government Affairs
> Pennsylvania Chamber of Business & Industry
> House State Government Committee Testimony
> March 19, 2013

We have zeroed in on the solution to the mystery of regulatory reform. The
analysis in Chapter Six provided some clues that politicians enact regulatory
reforms, despite little evidence that they lead to significant policy changes,
in order to create an avenue of influence on occasional regulatory decisions.
In Chapter Five, we saw that there is an overall sense that regulations, in
general, are a problem during bad economic times despite any a lack of specific dissatisfaction with particular rules. The quote above, drawn from testimony given before a legislative committee considering regulatory reform
in Pennsylvania on behalf of the state's largest business advocacy group
echoes this concern. This perception runs deep in both North Carolina and
Pennsylvania, two states where there are already myriad procedures created
with the intent of curbing regulation.

This perception indicates that it also may be the case that regulatory
reforms provide an easy way for politicians to demonstrate responsiveness
when economic times are difficult or particular constituents are unhappy
about regulation. It gives them the ability to appear responsive without actually repealing regulations and offending other constituents who support the
goals of regulation.

But this conclusion runs counter to many of the perceptions of regulatory
reform. Supporters of regulatory reforms argue that these procedures are
motivated by attempts to improve regulation and critics believe that they are
intentional efforts to make regulating so hard that agencies do not do so.
Scholars, as outlined in Chapter One, see regulatory reforms as empowering
constituencies (which constituencies vary with the theory of the regulatory

state), or allowing politicians to push regulatory decisions in the future in their preferred directions.

To make our conclusions about regulatory reform stronger, this chapter examines two states where it has run rampant. Arguably the regulatory processes in Pennsylvania and North Carolina are more complex and have more veto points than even the federal process. Our goal in this chapter is twofold. First, we hope to understand the motivation behind the creation of the regulatory environment in these two states. Second, we intend to use the functioning of these regulatory procedures to see how well the regulatory environment has met the goals of those who created it. Indeed, attempts at regulatory reform continue in the current sessions of the legislature in both states.

We find further corroboration for our arguments in Chapters Two and Three that regulatory reforms are largely epiphenomenal; that they don't have a significant impact on regulatory output. We also add significantly to the arguments in the previous two chapters. The perception that the volume of regulation is hurting business, shown with our survey of Midwestern states, is a significant factor in the political desire to enact regulatory reforms. Politicians in Pennsylvania and North Carolina have felt compelled to deal with this perceived problem of overregulation (even if regulatory reform doesn't really deal with it), particularly during times of economic stress. Regulatory reform also provides a convenient means for legislators or governors to intervene in regulatory decisions and, at a minimum, give the appearance of helping constituents.

This chapter is organized as follows. In Section 7.1, we discuss our selection of the two states and proceed to review the regulatory process in Pennsylvania, including previous assessments of this process. In Section 7.2, we discuss our interviews with the various actors involved in regulatory reform in Pennsylvania. We repeat these two themes for North Carolina in Sections 7.3 and 7.4. Section 7.5 offers concluding observations on these two states.

7.1 TWO STATES WITH MANY PROCEDURES

For the analysis in the preceding chapter, we gave each of the fifty states a score ranging from zero to ten for each of three categories. States were rated for the stringency of their executive review, legislative review, and economic analysis. The mean scores for the two review variables were both five and the mean analysis score was six. All three variables had values over the full range from zero to ten. For this chapter, our goal was to find states that had extensive procedures so as to better understand the reasoning for the continual passage of regulatory reforms.

Four states scored above a seven in each of the three categories. These states were Connecticut, North Carolina, Pennsylvania, and Wisconsin. Wisconsin barely crossed this threshold with a score of seven in each of the three categories. When we ranked the states on our scale, Pennsylvania and North Carolina had scores of twenty-seven out of thirty in terms of executive, legislative, and fiscal reviews, while Connecticut had a twenty-four.[1] We also wanted some geographic diversity among our states and chose Pennsylvania over Connecticut for our northeastern state because (as will be discussed further below) of the relatively unique body, the Independent Regulatory Review Commission (IRRC), and its higher overall score. This led us to choose studies of regulatory reform in Pennsylvania and North Carolina.

The case study approach (used in Chapter Three with New Jersey) allows the researcher to gain a deeper understanding of political processes and motivations. While it cannot be used to prove or disprove hypotheses, it adds texture to broader analyses and can be particularly useful for hypothesis generation. In these case studies we had several goals. First, we hoped to verify our earlier negative findings about the causes of regulatory reform (it cannot be explained by ideology, party control, or visions of the regulatory state). Second, we wanted to give support to the argument outlined in the previous two chapters: that politicians turn to regulatory reform for symbolic reasons (to look like they are doing something to help the economy) and to create a venue by which they can influence particular decisions without changing the overall regulatory output.

7.2 THE REGULATORY PROCESS IN PENNSYLVANIA

Pennsylvania subjects agency regulations to a wide variety of requirements. Several offices within the executive branch review regulations, although some of them are restricted to reviewing them for statutory compliance, including the Office of General Counsel (OGC). The Office of Planning and the Office of Budget, housed within the governor's office, conduct a review that extends to fiscal parameters and matters of policy. In each case, these reviews are limited to those agencies that report directly to the governor. Independent agencies are exempt from this review process but are subject to a review by the Attorney General, who holds a statewide elected position. Agencies are required to write a fiscal note analyzing the economic impact of their regulations. This requirement has recently been strengthened to include a more detailed examination of the impact of regulations on small businesses. Regulations also must be completed within two years of proposal. Most prominently and most uniquely, there is an Independent Regulatory Review Commission (IRRC) with members appointed by the legislature and the governor that reviews every agency regulation (except for hunting and gaming regulations). As one scholar put it, "Here under this system, we have one two-day review period, one seven-day review period, four ten-day review periods, two twenty-day review periods, two thirty-day review periods, and one forty-day review period," (Power 1999 p. 423).

The basic process for promulgating a regulation in Pennsylvania was set up in the Commonwealth Documents Law passed in 1968 and codified at 45 P.S. §§ 1201–1208. The process was reformed significantly in the early 1980s. The Commonwealth Attorneys Act passed in 1981 and codified at 71 P.S. §§ 732–204(b) and 732–301(10) brought review from the OGC and the Attorney General to the regulatory process. OGC reviews a rule to ensure:

- It is clearly drafted;
- The preamble satisfactorily explains the purpose of, need for, and statutory basis of the regulation; and
- The Regulatory Analysis Form is completed correctly.[2]

The Attorney General (AG) was given the power to review regulations for their legal content. The AG can hold regulations that it deems as raising legal concerns for up to thirty days, during which time it discusses those concerns with the agency. The AG can also "toll" a regulation, which in effect stops the clock while it waits for clarification from the agency on an issue raised by the office. If the objections are unresolved the agency may publish the regulation but must also publish the objections from the Attorney General.[3]

The legislature made a major modification to the regulatory process in 1982 with the passage of the Regulatory Review Act.[4] This act created the Independent Regulatory Review Commission (IRRC), which was charged with reviewing all regulations and making recommendations to the legislature. The IRRC reviews both proposed and final regulations.[5] The five members of the IRRC are appointed as follows: one each by the majority and minority leaders in each house of the Pennsylvania legislature and one by the governor.

The two primary standards for IRRC regulatory review are statutory authority and legislative intent, but the IRRC can also consider whether a regulation is in the "public interest," which includes an assessment of the economic and fiscal impact of the regulation. The legislature has added to the criteria over the years, including whether acceptable data is the basis of the regulation in 2011[6] and whether the agency has considered less costly alternatives in 2012.[7]

When the IRRC reviews the regulation at the proposed stage, it may choose to submit comments to the agency as part of the public comment process. Agencies must consider and respond to all comments they receive, including those from the public, the IRRC, and legislative committees. At the final stage, the IRRC (and the standing legislative committees) may approve or disapprove the regulation. If they both approve the regulation, it goes into effect. If the IRRC approves and the standing legislative committee disapproves, the committee may introduce a concurrent resolution before the legislature. If the legislature passes the resolution, and the governor signs it, then the rule cannot go into effect.

If the IRRC disapproves the regulation at one of its monthly public meetings, the agency has forty days to respond to the IRRC. They may modify the regulation, decide to proceed, or withdraw it. If they decide to modify or proceed with the regulation, the IRRC reconsiders it at its next meeting. If the IRRC again disapproves it, then the action moves again to the General Assembly, where a resolution may be introduced as in the above description. In order to invalidate a regulation, both houses of the legislature must pass the resolution and it must be signed by the governor.

By the 1990s, the governor's office was also getting into the act of regulatory reform. Executive Order 1996–1 required that all regulations must be reviewed by the governor's office, a requirement that in practice has been conducted by the governor's Director of Policy. As mentioned above, two other agencies in the executive branch, the Attorney General and the Office of General Counsel, also review rules, but unlike these offices, the scope of review by the Director of Policy is not restricted in its subject matter.

As this book went to press, three legislative proposals making changes to the state's regulatory procedures were introduced in the opening session of the Regular Session 2013–2014 of the PA General Assembly. HB 868 (Rep. Moul—R) would modify the Regulatory Review Act by amending definitions, and providing that if a standing committee of either legislative chamber disapproves of a regulation, an administrative agency may either withdraw the regulation or revise and resubmit the regulation. HB 211 (Rep. Grove—R) requires agencies to undergo a public interest analysis of their regulations every five years (a sunset provision of sorts). If it is determined that a regulation is not in the public interest, the legislation provides considerations the agency must undertake in its revision of the regulation. HB 549 (Rep. Scavello—R) allows for the review, upon petition of the General Assembly or the commission, of regulations by the commission that have been in effect for at least two years, instead of three years as currently prescribed by law.

Previous analyses of Pennsylvania's regulatory process are limited. The Institute for Policy Integrity report (Schwartz 2010), which briefly describes the regulatory process in each of the fifty states, gives Pennsylvania a "B-", which is actually one of its higher grades. It states, "The IRRC meets regularly and has clear standards for review. It promotes public participation, accepting and responding to public comments, and it can sometimes help calibrate regulations. But agencies feel the process is burdensome and subject to delays; similarly, there are no time limits on the reviews conducted by the General Counsel" (350).[8]

The IRRC has been the subject of some controversy since its inception. When it was originally created in 1982, the legislature also gave itself the ability to veto regulations disapproved by the IRRC with a bill passed by one house. This was changed to the current procedure in 1989[9] (soon afterwards the Pennsylvania Supreme Court ruled that the one house veto had been unconstitutional[10]), but some critics still argued that the IRRC was unconstitutional. Another criticism was that the IRRC provided an additional conduit for special interest influence over the regulatory process (Zambito 1997).

In an article evaluating regulatory review in Pennsylvania, Power (1999) presents two sides of the argument. On the one hand, the IRRC review in particular gives the legislature no powers that it doesn't already have, because in order to invalidate a regulation, a law signed by the governor (or passed over the governor's veto) is necessary. On the other hand, Power observes:

> the regulatory review process presents a structure for adversarial testing of administrative policies . . . with regulatory review, executive agencies cannot adopt regulations without having solid justification, without being prepared on the most difficult policy and fact issues, and without being flexible enough to make changes where appropriate. (450)

On balance, Power believes these benefits justify the delays imposed by the process.

7.3 REGULATORY REFORM IN PENNSYLVANIA

To gain an understanding of the motivations behind the various regulatory reforms in Pennsylvania and how they have actually functioned, we interviewed a series of people intimately involved with regulation in the Keystone State. We selected individuals who had a variety of perspectives, and who were involved with both the creation and implementation of regulatory procedures. We were fortunate to speak with several legislators involved with the passage of regulatory reforms in the early 1980s. We also spoke with former and current members and staff of the IRRC. We spoke with individuals who have served in the governor's office in various administrations and one person in the Attorney General's office. Finally, we spoke to representatives of regulatory agencies and interest groups that engage on regulatory issues. We spoke to a total of eighteen people.

We explained to each subject the nature of the project in broad terms. Consistent with recommended interview practice, we promised anonymity to interview subjects so they would feel comfortable speaking freely (Rubin and Rubin 1995). We asked each respondent for names and contact information of others who might be able to help us with this project. Questions for interview subjects varied with the position and area of expertise of the subject.

A number of themes emerged from the interviews that bear on the central question of why engage in regulatory reform. Two themes tended to dominate, both of which were discussed in Chapter Six. The first is that regulatory reform is a way to respond to complaints about regulation (either regulation in general or a regulation in particular) without revisiting the issue of the statutes underlying regulations and antagonizing the supporters of those statutes. The second is interbranch competition for the ability to influence regulatory decisions. This is particularly true in the origins of the IRRC, as legislators were very concerned about the governor's power to influence regulation, and in the increased regulatory growth as measured by the number of regulations annually adopted.

This is not to say that some proponents of regulatory reform do not couple purer motivations for improving regulations with the more cynical explanations given above. The belief that regulatory reform helps is a persistent one. This is true despite our findings in Chapters Two and Three, and more importantly despite the limited evidence that regulatory reform in Pennsylvania has served any purpose besides facilitating existing coalition influence on regulatory decisions. In particular, analytical requirements, review by the Attorney General and Office of General Counsel, and the ability of the legislature to overturn a regulation with a concurrent resolution have all appeared to have very limited policy consequences. The stories of the IRRC's influence and the role of the Policy Director are more complicated, but as we discuss below, the political influence of these requirements outweighs the policy influence. Notwithstanding a regulatory structure that is generally regarded positively by business advocacy groups and the lack of specific "overreaching" or "unfair" regulations, legislators today are searching for yet more regulatory reform mechanisms.

But before we get to the role currently played by these institutions, we should talk about their origins. We spoke with a number of legislators who played a role in the establishment of the IRRC in 1982. One theme that the legislators consistently voiced was that the creation of the IRRC was a response to overreaching by the governor and executive agencies. One interview subject said, "I think that the problem was that legislators began to complain about the governor (not a specific governor), as state government grew, governors did more with regulatory processes," while a former legislative staffer said, "But there had been, for several years, a growing feeling within the legislature, House and Senate, that agencies were creating their own policy through the regulatory process."

Richard Thornburgh (not an interview subject) was the Governor of Pennsylvania when the IRRC statute passed. Numerous interviewees mentioned that Thornburgh was "not excited" about the statute but that he ensured that a senior staffer was present throughout the negotiations on it. This was instrumental in the inclusion of an appointee from the governor on the IRRC (in fact, the governor's appointee is the tiebreaking member from a partisan standpoint, since the other four members are guaranteed to be evenly divided between Democrats and Republicans), and the absence of veto authority at the IRRC.

Another factor in Thornburgh's acquiescence to the imposition of the IRRC on an executive function such as rulemaking was the widespread sentiment about regulation in the early 1980s. The country was still in recession and President Reagan had campaigned on a theme of limiting government. According to numerous sources, there was strong antiregulatory sentiment in Pennsylvania during this period. One interview subject described that, "there was a clear sense that rules were being put in place that went beyond the law and had a severe impact on small businesses." Another responded to the question of who supported the IRRC bill by saying, "Support came from many sectors including business, local governments, school districts, and individual citizens, who were expected to hew to rules and regulations of the executive branch, which were often outside the statutory framework established by the state legislature."

So the establishment of the IRRC clearly was motivated both by legislators feeling powerless to influence a function they had delegated to the executive branch, and the need to respond to a business sentiment that regulation was a bad thing. This sentiment repeated itself during the next major recession in 2007–2009 and, not surprisingly, additional regulatory reforms were passed in Pennsylvania, expanding the analytical requirements in the 1982 statute to include more detailed examinations of regulatory impacts on small businesses. We suspect that this phenomenon is occurring again in the slow recovery following the Great Recession.

Another way to examine the intent behind the creation of a regulatory reform is to see how political actors and interest groups have used that reform once it is in place. To be certain, there are those who contend that the IRRC hews closely to its statutory criteria and ignores political influences.[11] One IRRC staff member argued that they simply focus on the statutory criteria. Another added, "We may receive a large number of public comments on a controversial or complicated proposed regulation. There may be a large number of commenters who are opposed to the regulation and only a few in favor of it. While our commissioners are interested in what the commenters have to say, they do not conduct a poll or count votes." Numerous people that we interviewed strenuously maintain that politics is not a factor at the IRRC. On the other hand, there was considerable sentiment that political influence does play a role in IRRC decision-making, particularly as perceived by those outside the commission. One executive office employee said, "I made it my job to know the Democrats on the IRRC so if I need to talk to them. They carry the water of their appointing authority. I knew the Republicans too but I knew they wouldn't vote our way. So, I knew that I had to get the D's to go along with me . . . I would twist arms if needed." An agency representative said, "Rather than do their own independent analysis, the IRRC would at times parrot the critiques of the House committee." Numerous respondents argued that the trend toward political influence at the IRRC has increased with time.

Both Democrats and Republicans we interviewed noted that some governors have used the IRRC to advance the governor's agenda. According to one Republican commissioner, he was invited to a cabinet meeting to "reinforce what the governor had run on . . . the agencies were there to put forth rules that the governor wanted, not what the agencies wanted." This comment immediately followed what one former legislator described as the time when "there was a general consensus from business . . . that regulations were overreaching and there were too many regulations." During a Democratic administration, one commissioner viewed his job as "being the eyes and ears of the governor."

And legislators will go to the IRRC to influence a particular decision (consistent with Fiorina's argument that institutions are created to facilitate casework for legislators). As one commissioner said, "We've had instances where a member has come in front of the commission at our meetings to talk about it. In one instance it was a prime sponsor who obviously carried a lot of weight regarding legislative intent, at least for me." Perhaps most revealing was a discussion with an interest group representative who acknowledged that if an agency was not being responsive to their concerns, they would go to a legislator and get them to submit a comment on a regulation to the IRRC. Because any issue could be framed as violating legislative intent, a legislator's comment to the IRRC appealing to this criterion is a particularly attractive mode of influence for an interest group.

Legislative intent was also important to the Republican commissioner who met with the governor's cabinet. Later in our interview, he emphasized that he "absolutely gives deference to legislative intent. Regulations only have the power the legislature gives them." While he commented that he was rarely was contacted by legislators, he did recount one story of a legislator in response to our question about whether the IRRC process could be usurped for purely political motives. He acknowledged that the IRRC "absolutely can be a shelter for the legislature. By writing a letter to the IRRC, it is a great way of showing a constituent I am fighting for you. It makes the constituent happy." He then shared this encounter:

> I once got a letter from a legislator and I happen to run into him at an event and mentioned that I had received his letter and was taking his concerns very seriously. He then told me, don't worry about what's in the [letter], I don't care what you do. He was actually surprised I was taking it seriously.

All the legislator cared about was the appearance of caring that the letter conveyed to his constituent.

All of the participants we interviewed agreed that the IRRC review subjects rulemaking in Pennsylvania to extensive scrutiny. One bureaucrat described the process as a "necessary evil" while another commissioner dismissed it as "simply delaying the inevitable." Many agreed that it offered stakeholders one last opportunity to express their concerns before a rule is adopted; this may create a perception of accountability within the regulated community. Still, many also acknowledged that policy-related decisions are made before a rule is ever proposed.

While there are differences of opinion on the role of the IRRC, there is greater consensus on the role of the analytical requirements imposed upon agencies. The motivation for the imposition of the original analytical requirements was similar to those that motivated the creation of the IRRC. A desire by the legislature to both satisfy business concerns about regulation (without repealing regulations) and gain an upper hand in the competition between the executive and legislative branches played a role. One former legislator said, "So we also required executive branch to be mindful of economic and social impacts. There were too many instances where executive departments like DER[12] got outside of what was reasonable and feasible."[13]

The goals of the analysis may have been similar to the goals of the IRRC, but the effect has been much more limited. Across the spectrum of our interview subjects, there was agreement that economic analysis done by the agencies was very limited, and played virtually no role in the selection of regulatory policy alternatives. One agency representative said, "but a lot of times the regulations we deal with, it's almost impossible to quantify any sort of fiscal impact or a numerical cost benefit," while another described the analysis as "pro forma." An interest group representative said that the analyses were "just describing what the rule does . . . there was no economics involved."

As for executive branch review, the role of the Policy Director, established by Executive Order 1996-1, varied considerably across administrations. One former Policy Director claimed to have read every word of every rule and seriously engaged agencies on specific rulemakings. This seemed to be more extensive involvement than in other administrations. For governors who want to play a role in regulatory policy, the Executive Order appears to give them the means to do so through the Policy Director. It is not clear, however, that it is necessary, as several interview subjects cited the governor's appointment power as an important means of influence.

The reviews by the Attorney General and Office of General Counsel (OGC), most parties agreed, are focused primarily on legal issues and the wording of regulations and rarely (if ever) delved into policy. As one agency representative said, "Typically, from my vantage point, they [AG] have a single person over there that reviews these regulations so their review is very focused within the scope of review and decided quickly," while another said, "For the most part, the AG did not assert its authority to stop a regulation." Interestingly, until 2013, all Pennsylvania Attorney Generals have been Republicans. The first Democratic Attorney General was elected in 2012. Whether this makes any difference in the role of the Attorney General's regulatory review will be interesting to observe.

Perhaps the best evidence of both the futility of past efforts of regulatory reform and the continuing appeal of regulatory reform as a policy option is the action in the current (2013) legislative session. As described above, regulatory reform has been a frequent topic of debate in this session. Legislative supporters of the reform recount vague stories of business owners who have complained to them about the number and cost of regulations in the state. Rather than amending or repealing laws, or less intrusively, intervening by offering comments or holding a hearing on a rule proposal as prescribed under the law, legislators are sponsoring new reforms.

Supporters of the current proposed measures in Pennsylvania are advocating for the pending legislation because it would "improve" the process, make "the process as transparent and open as possible,"[14] and "hold agencies accountable for outcomes."[15] However, these envisioned policy outcomes are unaccompanied by any evidence of similar success occurring in other states[16] (just that these procedures exist in other states) or any acknowledgement that Pennsylvania already has one of the most complex regulatory processes in the country.[17]

This is further evidence that regulatory reforms provide an easy way for politicians to demonstrate responsiveness when economic times are difficult or particular constituents are unhappy about regulation. The current legislation gives the sponsors the ability to appear responsive by voicing opposition to regulation and support of business without actually repealing regulations and offending other constituents who support the goals of regulation. Consider this exchange debating the merits of the three-bill package among members of the Pennsylvania House State Government Committee during an informational hearing held on April 4, 2013[18]:

> Rep. Brad Roae (R) said most of the complaints received by legislators are about various regulations . . . the purpose of the bills is to prevent new excessive regulations and get rid of the old ones that are no longer needed. Chairman Mark Cohen (D) countered that Rep. Roae can introduce bills to change those regulations . . . Citing his 25 years of experience in the private sector, Rep. David Maloney (R) commented: "In the private sector, this is the number one issue." He argued that bureaucrats must be "held accountable" and that the legislation would "bring them in line."[19]

Regulatory reform in Pennsylvania has either resulted in little change in regulatory substance (in the case of analysis and AG or OGC review) or has provided a venue for political actors to intervene in agency rulemaking (in the case of the IRRC and review by the Policy Director).[20] This latter result is consistent with the motivations of the legislators or the governor who enacted these requirements. The former result (or lack of result) may be consistent as well if one views the motivation of legislators as responding to generic concerns about regulation with some kind of action that won't actually offend any constituencies. Even those who may have noble goals in enacting regulatory reform may realize its limitations. One legislator that we interviewed summed the subject up eloquently: "I don't think there is any way to draw up a regulatory process without recognizing that politics is always going to play a role in this process. Even though I have reservations about this, I don't see how it can change."

7.4 THE REGULATORY PROCESS IN NORTH CAROLINA

Like Pennsylvania, the story of regulatory reform in North Carolina dates back to the 1980s. North Carolina has modified its regulatory process continually over the past few decades. And like Pennsylvania, despite a regulatory process that has one of the largest numbers of procedural requirements in the nation, the governor and the state legislature continue to enact new changes to the regulatory process. The newly elected governor, Pat McRory, has promised to make regulation one of his priorities.

We spoke to eleven individuals in researching the regulatory process in North Carolina. These included both civil servants and political appointees in the executive branch, staff members (and appointees) of the Rules Review Commission (RRC), interest group representatives, and former legislators active on regulatory issues. In addition, perhaps because of the continual changes that have taken place, there are nearly a half dozen academic articles that have looked at various aspects of the regulatory process in North Carolina. The findings of these articles are also discussed below. First, though, we present a brief history of regulatory reform in North Carolina.

As in most states, North Carolina saw an upsurge in regulatory activity in the 1970s. In 1977 the state legislature created a standing committee of legislators, the Administrative Rules Review Committee. In 1981, the committee was given the authority to object on the record but not veto rules.[21] In 1982, in *Wallace v. Bone*,[22] the North Carolina Supreme Court found that legislative vetoes were unconstitutional, short circuiting efforts to give the Administrative Rules Review Committee veto authority (Nichols 1987). In 1983, the governor was also given the authority to create a regulatory review commission, but Governor Hunt refused to appoint members.

Frustrated with the inability to establish regulatory review, the North Carolina legislature in 1983 repealed the state Administrative Procedures Act (APA) effective July 1, 1985 and set about recreating the regulatory process. A new APA was passed in 1985 and, among its many features, the most salient for the purposes of this analysis was the creation of a Rules Review Commission. The Commission (unlike the earlier Administrative Rules Review Committee) is made up of individuals appointed by legislative leaders, not legislators themselves. It is also housed in the executive branch of government (an attempt to deal with the objections raised in *Wallace v. Bone*).

The Rules Review Commission was given veto power over executive branch regulations in a further burst of regulatory reform in 1995 (Mitchell 2004). It is charged with reviewing rules according to the following criteria:

It is within the authority delegated to the agency by the General Assembly.
a. It is clear and unambiguous.
b. It is reasonably necessary to implement or interpret an enactment of the General Assembly, or of Congress, or a regulation of a federal agency.
c. The Commission shall consider the cumulative effect of all rules adopted by the agency related to the specific purpose for which the rule is proposed.

The actions of the Rules Review Commission have been challenged in court, but the North Carolina Supreme Court has declined to decide these cases on constitutional grounds and the RRC today continues as a fundamental part of the regulatory process in North Carolina.

Over the next two decades, there were numerous changes to the regulatory process.[23] The most significant changes occurred in the 1994 legislative session. The Joint Legislative Administrative Procedures Oversight Committee[24] was created to review rules (later, review was limited to rules on which ten individuals requested review[25]). Also, the APA was modified to require economic analysis on all rules with an impact of more than $5 million. The threshold for this requirement has been ratcheted down several times since its initial passage and currently stands at $500,000. The analysis, called a "fiscal note," continues to be a part of the regulatory process.

The executive branch in North Carolina has given the fiscal note more prominence. In 2010, Governor Perdue issued Executive Order 70. The order added a great deal of specificity to the contents of the fiscal note, mirroring to a large extent the federal Executive Order 12866, which governs regulatory impact analysis for federal agencies. The state E.O. also required an examination of existing rules to find candidates for repeal and reaffirmed the role of the Office of State Budget and Management (OSBM) to conduct review of fiscal notes and regulations on behalf of the governor.

Many of the requirements in E.O. 70 were codified in S.B. 781, and four other regulatory reform bills passed in 2011. This included review of regulations by the OSBM, specifications for the fiscal note, and the examination of existing rules. The bills also put restrictions on state environmental agencies, restricting their ability to use rulemaking to cases where they were explicitly required to by state or federal law or in emergency circumstances (these are known as the "Hardison amendments"). Governor Perdue vetoed SB 781, calling it unconstitutional,[26] but it was subsequently passed by the legislature over her veto.

Academic perspectives on the history of regulatory reform in North Carolina have been mostly critical. Although IPI's review of the state was mixed, giving it a "C+" grade but praising the analytical requirements, IPI criticized the transparency and delay associated with the process). Mitchell (2004) writes, "The administrative rulemaking process in North Carolina has engendered much contempt during the past several decades and repeated attempts at regulatory reform have done little but stoke the coals of an already fiery debate," and, "repeated increases in power granted to the RRC have done little to temper the frustration caused by the rulemaking process" (2092). Whisnant and DeWitt Cherry (1996) note that the statutes requiring economic analysis (at least prior to S.B. 781) were deliberately vague and may have been a tool for increasing legislative oversight over rulemaking. In defending the 1995 expansion of the RRC's power, Mitchell (1996) complains about North Carolinians "being strangled by bureaucratic red tape" (800).

As for the role of the RRC, Ballantine (2004) notes that "opponents of the RRC argue that the RRC provides a forum to re-argue policy issues with which agencies have already wrestled, and that the criteria used by the

RRC in reviewing rules are too vague, increasing the risk that the RRC will be able to paralyze agency action based on ideology and political pressure" (2102).[27] She also notes lingering doubts about RRC's constitutionality.

7.5 REGULATORY REFORM IN NORTH CAROLINA

The main theme that emerges from talking to people involved with regulation in North Carolina is constant change. One interview subject described the revisions as "comical" in their frequency . This constant change raises questions about the effectiveness of previous reforms. North Carolina provides further evidence of the inability of regulatory reform to meet the goals of its sponsors. One of the reasons that regulatory reform has been a constant theme is that prior regulatory reforms have not accomplished the goals of their enacting coalitions. There is, of course, more to the story than that, however. After briefly discussing our findings on many of the individual components of the North Carolina regulatory process, we will come back to this question.

The component of the regulatory process that has garnered the most attention is the Rules Review Commission (RRC). The origins of the RRC largely mirror those of the IRRC in Pennsylvania. Legislators were concerned about their lack of influence over executive branch rulemaking. One interview subject described the behavior of executive branch agencies as, "A lot of usurpation of power. Once you gave them power, they would reach out further." Also, like many regulatory reforms, both the initial creation of the RRC (and its predecessors) and the granting of veto authority over regulations to it were characterized as responses to general concern about the level of regulation in the state during the recession of the early 1980s.

As with the IRRC in Pennsylvania, perspectives varied somewhat on the role of the RRC in affecting regulatory policy. Those with experience, either as staff or as appointees to the RRC, generally stressed the fealty of the RRC to its statutory mandate to examine rules for compliance with legislative intent and clarity. One former commissioner said, "I looked at the guidelines that the legislature set up for the RRC to see if it came in our parameters. I tried to look at it from a citizen standpoint." Numerous parties agreed that long-term staff at the RRC helped "train" commissioners to understand the limits of their authority.

Outsiders noted that the RRC could be a venue for interest group influence, although unlike the IRRC, legislators did not appear to comment frequently on pending decisions. However, all parties (including a former member) agreed that the RRC had changed significantly in recent years. Most subjects attributed this to the GOP takeover of the state legislature in 2011 and the appointment of an entirely new slate of commissioners. One interest group representative said, "In recent years it has unilaterally promulgated policy in a way that overstates their authority," while a former commissioner described the change thusly: "one of the purposes [of the new appointments] was to allow those to create a friendlier atmosphere for Republican policies." One interview subject noted that some commissioners have met with legislative leaders, which never happened before this set of RRC appointees.

As described above, in addition to the RRC, there are provisions for review by the North Carolina legislature. Created at the same time as various incarnations of the RRC, the motivation for legislative review mirrors the motivations for the RRC: a desire to curb executive branch authority and a response to generalized concern about regulation. Legislative review has also been used frequently by opponents of regulation as "another bite at the apple." One interview subject described the process as, "That is another way that regulated entities can give feedback."

One person familiar with legislative review described the process as relatively cooperative between the legislature and agencies. The legislature rarely overturns an agency regulation but rather, after extensive discussions with the agency, passes bills with instructions to the agency on how to modify the regulation. Such bills have never been vetoed according to the recollections of this individual.[28]

The recession of the early 1980s led to the precursors to the RRC and legislative review. The recession of the 1990s played a role in the strengthening of these controls and the introduction of economic analysis of regulations. When the Great Recession hit, however, both branches of government moved quickly in the area of regulatory reform. Both Governor Perdue (elected in 2008) and the newly Republican-controlled legislature (elected in 2010) made highly publicized listening tours across the state to understand citizen concerns about regulation.

One former agency employee described the results of the listening tours as follows:

> Neither one of these processes identified many rules that people complained about. If you look at it, one thing is that people complained about the layering on of federal and state rules. A lot of time what people complained about weren't regulations; they were state laws, local ordinances, federal rules. A lot of people complained about the Charlotte tree ordinance. Of course people don't care where the problems are coming from.

Numerous respondents described the lack of specific responses from constituents regarding regulations. That said, respondents associated with the legislature emphasized the overall concern with regulation voiced by the public rather than the lack of specific complaints. Not surprisingly, the Democratic governor and the Republican legislature responded to the listening tours differently.

Governor Perdue's administration took some limited actions to repeal regulations. One interview subject told us that few rules were repealed. More significantly, Governor Perdue issued Executive Order 70 in 2010.

Describing the motivation for the E.O., one executive branch employee said, "It was the times, back in 2010, we heard a lot, a loud roar, about government keeping the economy from reviving. Regulations were hampering business." Another cited the role of the 2010 midterm elections.

The Executive Order, which strengthened the review by the OSBM and the requirements for economic analysis, is still in its relative infancy and therefore is hard to evaluate. One executive branch agency employee said that the E.O. resulted in improved analysis while another criticized it as "tying agencies in knots." We did not find examples of regulations altered by conducting an economic analysis, but it is clear that OSBM review is quickly becoming an integral part of the regulatory process. Whether it will lead to more economically desirable regulations or predominantly enforce the current governor's policy preferences will need to be determined across administrations. The federal Office of Information and Regulatory Affairs (OIRA), on which OSBM review is modeled, has often been accused of doing the latter at the expense of the former (Shapiro 2005).

A further complicating factor for evaluating E.O. 70 is the passage of S.B. 781. The legislative response to E.O. 70 was largely positive but did not, as Governor Perdue may have hoped, head off legislative modifications to the regulatory process. With Republicans taking control of the legislature in 2011, a series of regulatory reform bills were passed. We asked a number of our interviewees for the rationale for passing further regulatory reform in a state that already had legislative review, independent review, gubernatorial review, and economic analysis. One critic of S.B. 781 said it was "an attempt to stop environmental regulation," while a supporter said that the bills were necessitated by North Carolina's poor job creation record.

But perhaps the most interesting response came from a former legislator. He said,

> It's all a fulfillment of campaign rhetoric. The Republican campaign rhetoric is that businesses are overburdened by regulations and costs, never mind that pro-business Democrats have treated them just fine for decades. Then they come into office and find that the system is set up so that businesses aren't overly burdened. But they have to do something because they said so on the campaign trail. So they reform the process even more than the previous governor or legislator did.
>
> It reminds me we had a Democratic governor who ran as a prison reform lock 'em up candidate and he got into office and found it had already been done, so he had to build more prisons in order to seem like he was keeping his campaign promises.

This is not to discount the ideological motivations voiced by supporters or opponents of regulatory reform. However, this answer is more consistent with the data presented earlier that shows that most regulatory reforms are an ineffective way to attack regulation and the results of both the North

Carolina listening tours and our survey in Chapter Five that show limited opposition to actual regulations but considerable angst about the number of regulations.

The regulatory reform bandwagon continues to roll in North Carolina. A new regulatory reform committee has been created in the North Carolina House. A bill requiring regulations to sunset every ten years has been introduced in the House. Despite all this regulatory reform, one of the biggest supporters of reform in North Carolina was enthusiastic about the prospects for curbing regulation in the state because of something else entirely. He told us that he expected regulations to be less of a problem because for the first time since Reconstruction, North Carolina had a Republican governor and the GOP controlled both houses of the legislature. With that in place, we don't need the procedures nearly as much, he said.[29]

7.5 DISCUSSION

In North Carolina and Pennsylvania, we talked to many people with varying perspectives on regulation, the regulatory process, and regulatory reform. Some deeply believed that regulatory reforms had led to better regulations in their states. Others deeply believed that they had hurt public health by making it harder to issue regulations. Yet many, particularly those who were present at the creation of these reforms, acknowledged that they were largely reactions to tough economic times—recessions in the 1980s, 1990s, and 2000s.

The regulatory reforms in both states were sold as helping with job loss during these difficult times. However, in neither state were the statutes that led to the regulations repealed. In fact, except for some regulations in North Carolina that all sides acknowledged were long out of date and irrelevant to the question of job creation, neither state repealed individual regulations in order to improve economic conditions. If reducing regulation was the real goal of regulatory reform, then one would expect that measures like this would at the very least be accompanied by rollbacks in regulation, not just reforms to the process for writing regulations.

And particularly in North Carolina, regulatory reform has followed regulatory reform, buttressing the argument that the previous reforms did not accomplish the goal of easing regulatory burdens. Even in Pennsylvania, where there had been little regulatory reform following the creation of the IRRC, recent years have seen increased analytical requirements and renewed attention from the both the governor's office and the state legislature since the onset of the Great Recession. In both states, the desire for more regulatory reform raises questions about the efficacy of the last round of reform (and about why anyone should expect that this time will be different).

The reforms that are in place have been used at least as often for political goals as for policy ones. Interest groups in Pennsylvania know that if they want to influence the IRRC, they should get a legislator to weigh in on a regulation that the IRRC is considering. Even the RRC in North Carolina, which has been praised for staying within its mission for two decades, has shown recent signs of providing an additional venue for legislators to deliver preferred policies to their constituents. Gubernatorial review in Pennsylvania and legislative review in North Carolina were both cited as additional ways that interest groups can try to re-litigate issues they may have lost at the agencies. In both of these states, the politics of regulatory reform has been more about politics than about regulation.

8   The *Politics* of Regulatory Reform

Regulatory reform is hot. While many of the reforms discussed in this book first made their appearance in the recessions of the late 1970s and early 1980s, the Great Recession has witnessed an unprecedented level of regulatory reform (both enacted and proposed). Dozens of regulatory reform bills have been put forth in the United States Congress over the past two sessions. As has been discussed in the preceding chapters, states across the nation have passed new regulatory reform measures that have widely varied in their form and content over the past decade.

But why? The empirical literature on procedures imposed upon regulatory agencies is quite dubious about the effectiveness of these procedures. Even notice and comment, hailed in the 1960s as a great innovation (Davis 1969), is now derided as Kabuki theater (Elliott 1992). The existing literature focuses largely on the impact of regulatory reform on the federal level. In Chapters Two and Three, we reaffirmed that literature on the state level. The intensity and volume of regulatory procedures enacted to constrain agency discretion seems to bear no relationship to the number of regulations agencies issue. Instead, the same politicians who enact regulatory reforms appear to already have considerable influence over agency regulatory output. More regulations are issued when Democrats control the legislature than when Republicans do.

If one listens to the rhetoric surrounding regulation, one could come up with a simple answer to the question of "Why regulatory reforms?" According to this rhetoric, regulations have such an outsize impact on our economy that even the smallest impacts (perhaps even undetectable impacts) on them would reverberate throughout the economy. So why not try regulatory reform? As we discussed in Chapter Four, existing studies of the macroeconomic effects of regulation have not been as clear as the rhetoric would have you believe. Instead, regulations have ambiguous impacts on employment and economic well-being, arguably improving them as often as harming them.

But the rhetoric is not unimportant. In Chapter Five we discovered that despite little data-based evidence in five Midwestern states that recent regulations had hurt employment or other economic conditions, a widespread perception exists among business owners that regulations were hurting them.

There was also an inability of business owners to name specific regulations that were of concern. This was echoed in North Carolina, where one of our interview subjects described how the statewide effort to find regulations that should be repealed came up with very few specific suggestions.[1] One is left with the impression that the continual effort by state and national politicians to emphasize the burden of regulations has resulted in a widespread perception that there are too many regulations.

Chapters Six and Seven explored the mystery of regulatory reform in more detail. Our examination of the data from all the states and more detailed studies of two states in particular led us to two solutions for this mystery. The first explanation is political position taking and the second is constituent service. Each of these explanations finds its mooring in theories of legislative behavior that are several decades old. They are detailed in the next two sections. We follow that up by revisiting the relationship between regulatory reform and theories of the regulatory state and a few parting words of advice for advocates and scholars evaluating regulatory reform initiatives.

8.1 CAUSING A PROBLEM AND THEN SEEKING CREDIT FOR SOLVING IT

A generation ago, David Mayhew (2004) argued that "politicians often get rewarded for taking positions rather than achieving effects" (xv). Mayhew describes two of the actions that politicians take to help ensure their reelections as "credit claiming" and "position taking." We believe that regulatory reform is an example of both of these phenomena. In this section, we discuss "position taking," and we turn to "credit claiming" below.

Severe economic downturns pose a significant problem for political officeholders. The ability of government to reverse a downturn and speed a recovery is at best limited, and how to do so is the subject of considerable dispute among both politicians and economists. Yet as a downturn occurs and lingers, the public is likely to blame those in office for their own reduced economic standing. In both the late 1970s/early 1980s recession and in the recent Great Recession, politicians have scapegoated regulation as the source of economic malaise. It is not a coincidence that these two periods have shown the greatest increase in the passage of regulatory reforms.

The claim that regulation has hampered the economy works because it is plausible. Regulation constrains the possible activities of business and, in doing so, may lead some businesses to fire employees or become less productive. As described in Chapter Four, some studies have found negative impacts of regulation on the economy. And in Chapter Five, we describe the possibility that regulations may have a larger impact during economic downturns. But other studies have found little impact or even positive impacts. And more importantly, when compared to other economic factors, such as reduced demand, globalization, and the collapse of the housing market, most economists agree that regulation is not a significant contributor to the state of the economy. But those other factors are much harder for politicians to fix.

So politicians blame regulation. But if one is going to blame regulation, then one has to have a plan to plausibly fix regulation. We note in Chapter Two that the factor that correlates best with a high regulatory output is Democratic control of the state legislature. The most plausible explanation for this correlation is that Democrats are more likely to pass laws that require agency regulation. In our five Midwestern states, the number of laws passed correlated with the number of regulations. It stands to reason that the best way to reduce regulation would be to repeal those laws. Yet those laws often pass because they have considerable public support. Repealing them would entail absorbing a political cost. There are very few examples of Congress or state legislatures repealing major regulatory statutes or ordering agencies to rescind particular regulations implementing those statutes.[2] Similarly, in Pennsylvania, where legislators have the authority under existing law to request a priority review of any regulation that has been on the books for three or more years, these reviews are rarely requested.

Still, politicians turn to regulatory reforms. Regulatory reforms allow elected officials to go back to the constituencies that are upset about the generic number of regulations (perhaps because those same politicians convinced them that they should be upset) and tell them that something is being done. This "something" could be enhanced oversight of renegade agencies that issue the regulations. It could be ensuring a process where business sits at the table when regulations are formulated. It could be a requirement that agencies ensure that the costs (particularly the compliance costs for business) of the regulations do not exceed the benefits. Any of these measures, politicians assure their supporters, will fix the "problem" of too much regulation.

Except that they don't. With a few exceptions (discussed below), regulatory reforms have at most a small effect on a small number of regulations. This has been the predominant finding of the academic literature. Public comment does not lead to more popular or responsive regulations (Golden 1998, West 2004). Analytical requirements do not lead to regulations that maximize net benefits or minimize costs (Shapiro and Morrall 2012). And while gubernatorial and legislative review are nice aids for executives and legislators to oversee bureaucrats, the data in Chapter Two show that other traditional tools, such as budgetary control, appointment power, and, most importantly, the power to pass legislation, may work just as well (Wood and Waterman 1991). The data in Chapter Two also show that none of these requirements affect the number of rules issued by a state which casts further doubt both on the effectiveness of regulatory reforms, and on the claim that they cripple the regulatory process.

The exceptions, the regulatory reforms that seem to make a difference, are important to note. Deadlines for completing a final rule, once proposed, do seem to depress rulemaking outcomes. A combination of a deadline and stringent executive review makes it particularly difficult for agencies to complete rules. A deadline is (usually) an absolute requirement. It can't be manipulated by existing coalitions of politicians or by agency officials in the way that analytical requirements, participation, or political oversight can be. This absolute quality of deadlines (either the rule comes out by the deadline or it doesn't) may differentiate them from other procedural controls. As shown in New Jersey, however, it may compromise the effectiveness of other controls. A rulemaking deadline in New Jersey appeared to make it less likely that agencies would respond to public comments on their proposals.

This absolutist quality also indicates other possible successful efforts to influence regulatory output. Requirements in organic statutes that agencies issue rules obviously increase rulemaking. Prohibitions on rulemaking, whether they are legislative, like the Hardison amendments discussed in Chapter Seven that severely restricted environmental rules in North Carolina, or executive, like the recent moratorium on regulations issued by Governor Mike Pence of Indiana discussed in Chapter Five, decrease rulemaking.

In Indiana, though, it is still too early to draw conclusions about the effectiveness of the moratorium. After four months into the Pence Administration, the number of rules adopted is comparable to that of his predecessor in his first four months of office. The real test will be to compare the level of rulemaking after the first twelve months of the governor's term, presuming the moratorium is not lifted. In similar instances where governors used executive orders to curtail rulemaking, the results have been muted after the governor's first year. Similarly, attempts to review and repeal existing regulations have had limited effects.[3]

But these absolute approaches are the exception. Indeed, even these approaches do not reduce the number of regulations; they merely prevent future regulations. It is the current stock of regulations that is the problem cited in much of the political rhetoric and in the responses to our survey. One is forced to conclude that a significant part of the motivation behind regulatory reforms is not their effectiveness. It is instead a desire to "do something" about the purported problem with regulations. It is "position seeking," as described by Mayhew. As one North Carolina legislator so aptly described it, "A politician comes in with anecdotal evidence about how they are overregulated and it becomes gospel on the campaign trail. Then they get into office and have to do something but realize it isn't like they said it was; but they have to do something."

8.2 PROVIDING A MECHANISM FOR CONSTITUENT SERVICE

It is tempting to be satisfied with the "position seeking" explanation for regulatory reform. But there is one nagging question. While we have shown that regulatory reforms have no significant large-scale impacts on the level of regulation, there are anecdotes of instances where a regulatory reform (such as the Independent Regulatory Review Commission in Pennsylvania) has made a difference in an occasional regulatory decision. One could brush this off as a few random events that do not reflect the broader story about regulatory reform.

Instead, we believe these are instances of a phenomena that Fiorina described in his works on Congress and bureaucracy in the 1970s and 1980s (these works are an expansion of Mayhew's "credit claiming"). Fiorina argued that Congress creates bureaucracies in order to create a mechanism for the delivery of benefits to citizens. Then, when a citizen is dissatisfied with the bureaucracy, the member of Congress can intervene on his or her behalf and receive credit from the citizen that will turn into a vote on Election Day.

Creating bureaucracies that regulate citizens or businesses could easily function the same way. A business is upset with a particular proposed regulation that imposes a burden upon it. It complains to its representative in Congress or the state legislature. The legislator can secure support from the business (either a vote or future campaign contributions) by intervening on its behalf to stop the regulation. There are some traditional methods for doing this, such as threatening the agency's budget, holding an oversight hearing, or inserting a prohibition on the proposal into another piece of legislation. Similarly, governors have multiple methods for influencing agency regulatory decisions (although perhaps fewer besides firing their appointee, which comes with a political cost).

But regulatory reforms may be more efficient ways of facilitating political interventions in agency regulatory decisions. Participation requirements allow a legislator to be heard on an issue, and agencies likely pay more attention to legislative comments than other public comments. Even if the comments don't result in a change, filing a comment shows a constituent that the legislator cares about her concerns. Review, either by a political body or an ostensibly independent body, gives the politician another body before which to argue the case of a constituent. Members of the IRRC in Pennsylvania readily acknowledged that they pay considerable attention to legislative appeals. Even an analytical requirement forces agencies to disclose more information about the impact of their regulations, which facilitates political intervention.

If politicians successfully use regulatory reform to reverse an agency proposal (or promote it), then the interested party that asked them to do so will be grateful. Even if the intervention is not successful, however, the constituent will have seen his or her representative pull every possible lever in order to help him or her, as noted by one IRRC commissioner in Pennsylvania in Chapter 7. This is also likely to result in an electoral benefit to the politician.

Fiorina advanced his hypothesis to explain the increasing bureaucratization of government. But what does the creation of additional regulatory procedures accomplish besides adding to the bureaucratization of the policy-making process? Every regulatory reform (again, except for the absolute ones) adds steps to the rulemaking process. In other words, it makes this process more bureaucratic. If Fiorina's argument has explanatory power for the increase of federal agencies, it is conceptually straightforward to extend it to the increased bureaucratization inherent in regulatory reforms.

The data in Chapters Six and Seven emphasize this point. Executive review is added more often in states that experience divided government. Presumably this is because governors of one party want to intervene in regulations promulgated pursuant to statutes passed by the opposing party. Executive review, along with requirements for analysis, occurs more often in states with more professional legislators. Governors feel they need more tools at their disposal to oversee regulators when the legislature is more capable of oversight. The case studies in Pennsylvania and North Carolina both present examples of this phenomenon. Members of supposedly neutral regulatory review bodies acknowledge giving greater weight to interventions in particular regulatory issues by legislators. Interest groups in both states know this and get legislators to write comments on their behalf advocating for a position in a regulatory decision. In some ways, the IRRC is statutorily obligated to "prioritize" these legislative comments. As one commissioner framed it, "the legislature is our natural constituency because they created us for a reason. We're here doing [their] job [when it comes to ensuring regulations mirror legislative intent]."

Regulatory reforms are often trumpeted as solving the problem of regulation (whatever that problem might be). However, they do very little to affect the overall volume of regulation and only occasionally seem to affect the substance of regulations. Instead, they are intended to solve a different problem. Elected officials, having complained about regulation and the burden it imposes on business and the economy, find themselves in office needing to do something about regulation. With few exceptions they don't want to repeal regulations or, more importantly, the underlying statutes that often reflect broadly held goals for improving public health. Regulatory reforms are the solution to this problem.

8.3 REGULATORY REFORM AND THEORIES OF THE REGULATORY STATE

In Chapter One, we outlined numerous theories of the regulatory state. Public choice theory argues that regulation serves powerful organized interests. Neopluralists see regulation as the output of interest group competition. To varying degrees, advocates of deliberate democracy, civic republicans, and expertocratic decision-making all see regulation as serving the broader public interest. It is tempting and even logical to fit regulatory reforms into these theories. And indeed the rhetoric surrounding regulatory reform reinforces this temptation. Opponents of regulatory reform (often those who find themselves voicing a public interest view of regulation) see these reforms as ways of allowing powerful interests to thwart the public interest.

We believe that regulatory reform is better explained by theories of political behavior (many of which were designed to explain legislative behavior, but we believe that they extend to executives as well) than by theories of the regulatory state. These theories advanced by Mayhew (2004) and Fiorina (1989) explain that holders of political office are primarily interested in advancing their reelection efforts. It then follows that the choices made by officeholders are intended to either serve their constituents or appear to do so. One way to do this is to support the bureaucratization of government so as to make the services of legislators or governors more necessary. Another way to do so is to claim to reduce the bureaucratization while in fact abetting it. This is where regulatory reform comes in.

The rhetoric surrounding regulatory reform is uniformly high-minded. Advocates argue that these reforms will make regulation smarter or more responsive to the public. They may argue that they will reduce unwanted regulation. Having spoken to many officials, we don't doubt that some believe that regulatory reforms will or do achieve these lofty goals. But the data (and not just our data but repeated studies of the federal regulatory process) tell a different story. While it is easy to find an occasional anecdote of regulatory reform "killing" a regulation, more often the reform takes the blame for the underlying preferences of the executive or the legislature. If legislators and governors put regulatory reforms in place to kill, slow, or improve regulation, they do so in the face of considerable evidence that reforms make little significant difference in regulation.

Instead, regulatory reform reflects the desire of politicians to get credit for improving the economy when few actual levers exist for them to achieve this task. It reflects their desire to take action on an issue that they themselves may be responsible for creating (concern about the level of regulation). There is no discernible pattern between the enactment of regulatory reform at the state level and the level of regulation in the state. Nor do patterns exist between party control of legislatures and executives and the enactment of reforms. Instead, regulatory reforms hold a somewhat universal appeal to politically motivated legislators and governors.

Regulatory reforms do not even seem to hold the potential voiced for them by political scientists who argued that they give the coalitions that enact them power over future regulatory decisions. Instead, the argument made by Horn and Shepsle (1989) that such reforms give future coalitions power to intervene in bureaucratic decisions seems more consistent with the evidence. Regulatory reforms have more to do with the politics of symbolism and credit claiming than with the politics of regulation. This is why the literature that endeavors to explain political behavior is more relevant to regulatory reforms than the literature that focuses on regulation.

While regulatory reforms seem to do little to improve regulations, it could also be argued that they do little to harm them. Indeed, the arguments about the ossification of the rulemaking process due to proceduralization seem also to be refuted by the lack of a relationship between regulatory volume and regulatory reform. But those considering regulatory reform should keep two things in mind. First, any policy solution that doesn't do what it claims, erodes faith and increases cynicism about government overall. Every time a regulation is passed despite promises from politicians that they have slowed or stopped regulation is another failure of government to deliver on its promises.

Second, regulatory reforms add unnecessary complexity to the process of governance and in doing so may make policy-making less accessible to citizens in the name of making it more accessible. Fiorina and Noll (1978a) argued, "legislators and bureaucrats have an incentive to provide government services in an excessively bureaucratized manner" (257). Regulatory reform is the result of these incentives despite rhetoric that claims that it is the solution to them.

Debates about regulatory reforms should take place with the understanding that they are indirect methods of arguing about regulation itself. The trade-off between improving public health and imposing costs on businesses is a real one, but it should be debated directly rather than through procedural changes that are unlikely to have much of an impact on regulations. Those who care about regulations should view reforms with skepticism and always ask the question: Why add this change to the regulatory process when none of the previous ones we added seemed to make a difference?

Appendix 1

Scales for Legislative Review, Executive Review, and Impact Analysis

EXECUTIVE REVIEW

Who conducts the review?

No one (0)
Within agency only (1)
Outside agency if triggered (2)
Mandatory outside agency (3)

Is review binding?

No (0)
Yes (1)

Who is the outside reviewer?

No one (0)
AG or independent agency (1)
Governor's office (2)

Criteria for review?

1 point for each for
    Procedural
    Legality
    Economic
    Others

LEGISLATIVE REVIEW

Nature of review

None (0)
Some regulations (1)
All regulations (2)

Nature of oversight

None (0)
Advisory (1)
Need full vote in both chambers to overturn (2)
Need full vote in one chamber to overturn (3)
Committee can overturn (4)

Criteria for review

None (0)
Violates state Administrative Procedure Act APA (1)
Other legal problem or conflict (2)
Impact on certain communities (3)
Any policy reason (4)

IMPACT ANALYSIS

When is analysis done?

None (0)
If requested by legislature or governor (1)
If requested by public (2)
If $ threshold for effect on budget (3)
If $ threshold for effect on economy (4)
All regulations (5)

Types of impact analyzed

None (0)
On governments (1)
On private sector (2)

Who reviews analysis?

Within agency (0)
Independent review (1)

Scope of review

None (0)
Minimal (1)
Comprehensive (2)

Appendix 2

Survey Instrument for Midwestern Business Leaders

(Modifications in other modes noted below.)

Thank you for your help with this national business study being conducted by Rutgers, The State University of New Jersey. We have invited a small group of business leaders in five Midwestern states to participate, so your answers are very important to us. This survey should take only about five to seven minutes to complete.

If you agree to answer the questions on this survey, your answers will be confidential, that is, we will not release your individual answers to anyone. Your name or that of your company WILL NOT be recorded with your responses, BUT we may report your responses combined with those of others. Your participation is voluntary, you may end at any time, and you may skip questions you do not want to answer.

S1. Would you like to go to the first question now?

    1   YES

    0   NO → Attempt covert or Terminate

S2. Please enter your access code below.

Q1. First, we would like to start by asking you a couple questions about the general business climate in your state.

How would you rate the business climate in your state over the past five years? Would you say it has been excellent, good, fair, or poor?

    1   Excellent

    2   Good

    3   Fair

    4   Poor

    5   Don't know

Q2. Do you think your state's business climate will get better, worse, or stay the same over the next five years?

1   Get better

2   Get worse

3   Stay the same

4   Don't know

Q3. For each of the following issues, please indicate whether you agree or disagree that this is an important area of concern for your business right now?

	Strongly agree (1)	Somewhat agree (2)	Somewhat disagree (3)	Strongly disagree (4)	Don't know (5)
Weak customer demand	○	○	○	○	○
Cost of employee health benefits	○	○	○	○	○
Number of government regulations	○	○	○	○	○
Amount of taxes you pay	○	○	○	○	○
Complying with government regulations	○	○	○	○	○
Lack of credit availability	○	○	○	○	○
Quality and skills of workers	○	○	○	○	○
Uncertainty about future regulations	○	○	○	○	○

Q3A. Of those concerns that you strongly agree are an important area of concern, which ONE is the most important?

Q4.   We have listed some proposals recently being talked about to help businesses grow and improve the economy.

After you read the entire list, please tell us HOW MANY of these proposals you STRONGLY AGREE will help your business. By STRONGLY AGREE, it means you generally agree that the proposal will improve your business.

Please DO NOT tell us which ones you generally agree with—only HOW MANY:

- Eliminating incentives for employers to move jobs overseas
- Increasing consumer purchasing power
- Improving infrastructure like roads, bridges, and water systems
- Making more credit available for businesses
- Reducing the number of regulations (NOT AN OPTION IN THE CONTROL GROUP)

  1 Zero

  2 One

  3 Two

  4 Three

  5 Four

  6 Five

Q5. How much do you think that the number of regulations has contributed to the economic slowdown over the past five years in the United States? Do you think it has been a major or minor factor or none?

  1 Major factor

  2 Minor factor

  3 Not a factor

  4 Don't know

Q6. I am going to read you a short list of several kinds of regulations. Of these, please tell me which kind of regulations has had the MOST significant impact on the state's economy.

  You may indicate MORE than one kind of regulation.

  1 The number of government regulations

  2 Civil fines and noncompliance regulations

  3 Environmental compliance regulations

  4 Licensing regulations

  5 Employee benefit regulations

  6 Fee generating regulations

  7 Other kinds of regulations (PLEASE SPECIFY) _____

Q7. Compared to other business priorities in your state, how high a priority should it be for the state legislature and governor to focus on reducing

the number of regulations in your state? Should it be a high priority, a
medium priority, or a low priority?

1   High priority
2   Medium priority
3   Low priority
4   Don't know

Q8. Generally speaking, has the business climate in your state been made better
or worse by governmental regulations in your state, or no difference?

1   Better
2   Worse
3   No difference
4   Unsure

*LONGER WEB-BASED VERSION INCLUDED A BATTERY OF STATE-
MENTS TO WHICH RESPONDENTS WERE ASKED IF THEY AGREED
OR DISAGREED.

	Strongly agree (1)	Somewhat agree (2)	Somewhat disagree (3)	Strongly disagree (4)	Don't know (5)
Some regulation of business is necessary for a modern economy.	○	○	○	○	○
My business can live with some regulation if it is fair, manageable, and reasonable.	○	○	○	○	○
My business can live with some regulation, but there is too much right now in the current economy.	○	○	○	○	○
We should get rid of all government regulation on business.	○	○	○	○	○
Some regulations are important to protect small businesses from unfair competition and to level the playing field with big business.	○	○	○	○	○

Q9. Please tell me which of these statements comes closer to your own views—even if neither is exactly right.

   1   Government regulation of business is necessary to protect the public interest.

   2   Government regulation of business usually does more harm than good.

Q10. Again, which comes closer to your own views.

   1   Reducing the number of regulations is the best way to create jobs in the U.S.

   2   The number of government regulations is not the biggest factors impacting my business.

We are almost finished now.

**LONGER WEB-BASED VERSION INCLUDED PROBES ABOUT FIVE STATE-SPECIFIC LAWS AND REGULATIONS.

Q11. From your perspective, of the recent laws adopted in your state, which law has had the MOST impact on your business operations? Please skip if you cannot recall a recent state regulation impacting your business.

Q12. Also from your perspective, which regulation has had the MOST impact on your business operations in recent years? Please skip if you cannot recall a recent state regulation impacting your business.

Finally, I have just a few more questions for statistical purposes, which will help ensure that our sample is representative of business leaders in your state.

D1. What is your position in your company?

   1   CEO, CFO, CLO, COO, president

   2   Director or vice president

   3   Manager

   4   Owner or partner

   5   Other (PLEASE SPECIFY) _____

D2. Approximately how many people work 30 hours or more per week at your company, including yourself. Please provide your best estimate and DO NOT include contractors.

   1   Self-employed

   2   2–5 employees

   3   6–20 employees

   4   21–99 employees

    5   100–499 employees

    6   500 or more employees

D3. How long has your business been in operation?

    1   0–5 years

    2   6–10 years

    3   11–20 years

    4   Over 20 years

D4. For statistical purposes only, which of these categories best describes the GROSS revenue of your business in 2011?

    1   Under $250,000

    2   $250,000 to $500,000

    3   Over $500,000 to $1 million

    4   Over $1 million but under $10 million

    5   Over $10 million

D5. In what ZIP code is your business located.

****LONGER WEB-BASED VERSION INCLUDED TWO QUESTIONS ASKING ABOUT OPERATIONS OUTSIDE THE STATE AND COUNTRY.

D6. And lastly, do you generally think of yourself as a:

    1   Democrat

    2   Independent

    3   Republican

    4   Other (PLEASE SPECIFY) _____

D7. Please indicate your gender.

    1   Male

    2   Female

This completes our survey.

Thank you very much for your time and cooperation. If you have any questions, you may contact Dr. Stuart Shapiro or Dr. Debra Borie-Holtz at 848–932–5475. If you have any questions about your rights as a research participant, you may contact the administrator of the Rutgers Institutional Review Board at 848–932–0150. We would be happy to send you a copy of the final survey results for your state if you would like to provide us with your email at this time.

Have a good day and thank you again for your participation.

Appendix 3
Survey Methodology

Participants for the survey of Midwestern business executives were randomly selected from a sample frame of for-profit and non-profit firms operating in the five-state region, of which nine out of ten businesses were for-profit entities. The survey was administered in mixed modes: Email invitations were first sent to businesses to participate online. The initial poll contained thirty-eight closed-ended questions and five state-specific questions. Of the total, five were open-ended questions. Expecting that the survey length might affect response rates, the fourth and fifth contact attempts utilized a version of the instrument that reduced the state-specific and open-ended questions. About half of the sample completed the longer version. Telephone and facsimile surveys were targeted to those in the sample frame without emails; these modes utilized the shorter version of the instrument.

The Eagleton Center for Public Interest Polling, Rutgers University, completed the telephone portion of the survey. The survey was in the field from January to May of 2013.

The sample consists of n=387 business executives, managers, and professionals operating establishments within Illinois, Indiana, Michigan, Minnesota, and Wisconsin. The sampling error for respondents is ±4.9 percent, at a ninety-five percent confidence interval. Sample error does not take into account other sources of variation inherent in public opinion studies, such as coverage non-response, question wording, or question placement context effects. Column totals may not sum to 100% due to rounding.

The sample was stratified by state and then by North American Industry Classification System (NAICS) code to ensure a representative sample of industries by state. The sample was weighted by state to ensure it was representative of the proportion of business establishments operating in each state. Respondents represented businesses across the spectrum in terms of size, gross revenues, and time in operation. All the respondents held top management positions, including forty percent who were CEOs and CFOs or company presidents, while another forty percent were the partner or owner of the establishment. Nineteen percent of respondents were self-employed, thirty-two percent had two to five employees, twenty-eight percent had six to twenty, fourteen percent had twenty-one to ninety-nine employees, and nine percent had 100 or more employees; the median number of employees was six to twenty.

More than half (54%) of the business executives interviewed said they have been operating in business for over twenty years, a quarter have been in business for more than a decade, while nineteen percent have been in operation for less than ten years. Gross revenues for those surveyed were also proportional across the sample, with thirty percent earning over $1 million. Twenty percent earned between $250,000 and $500,000 and 20 percent between $500,000 to just under a million dollars. About a quarter reported earnings less than $250,000. Overall, seventy-one percent were male and twenty-nine percent of all respondents were female.

We were also guided by national polling conducted in the last decade for some of our questions. Additionally, we tested the reliability of the survey instrument by randomly assigning the web-administered interviewees to two different survey landing pages. Identical surveys were administered, with the exception of one experimental question. To help ensure reliability, we then compared the answers of respondents by question to see if there were differences in the responses; we found no statistical differences between respondents in either group for any of the questions asked.

Given the potential context effects associated with the concept of regulatory burden within the business community, we thought it was important to gauge whether respondents had an overall perception about regulations at the start of the survey. No doubt the term "government regulation" has become so infused in our political rhetoric that the mere mention of the concept is likely to conjure up both positive and negative mental images. To look at this potential effect, we employed a list-experiment technique in our web survey design. Before we asked about regulations and their impact on businesses, we included a list-type question in order to avoid measurement errors that arise when asking about politically infused issues that may introduce bias. The difference in the mean scores on this question represents the percentage of those who perceived "regulations as a concern" at the start.

Finally, the verbatim wording of all questions asked is reproduced as Appendix 2. With the exception of the experimental question and those with ordinal values, the response categories were also randomized.

Appendix 4
State Ranking of Regulatory Reform Scale

State	SUM	AZ	AR	DE	ID	IL	IN	IA	KS	LA	ME	MI	MN	MO	MT	NV	NH	NJ	NM	NY	NC	OK	PA	SD	TN	VA	WA	WI	WY
Executive Review Score	10	9	5	0	0	0	0	8	0	10	4	10	10	0	8	6	0	4	0	9	8	6	10	0	0	8	0	7	8
Legislative Review Score	10	0	7	0	5	10	4	8	2	7	5	4	4	6	6	8	6	5	0	3	9	8	7	9	10	4	4	7	6
Economic Impact Score	10	7	4	0	6	3	9	6	8	7	6	10	1	4	7	5	8	7	0	10	9	5	10	6	6	10	7	7	0
Response to Comments (0 - not required, 1 - required)	1	1	0	1	0	0	0	0	0	1	1	0	0	0	1	0	1	1	0	1	0	0	1	0	0	0	1	1	0
Time Deadlines for Rulemaking Process (0 - no deadline, 1 - deadline)	1	0	0	1	0	1	1	1	0	1	1	1	1	1	1	0	1	1	0	0	1	1	1	1	1	0	0	0	1
Sunset Provision for Rules (0 - no sunset, 1 - sunset)	1	1	0	1	1	1	1	0	0	1	1	1	0	0	1	1	1	1	1	1	0	1	1	1	0	1	1	1	0
Non-Economic Impact Statements (Number Required)	8	2	1	0	0	1	1	1	2	2	1	1	1	2	2	1	1	6	0	2	0	2	1	1	1	2	1	1	0
Non-Economic Impact Statements (0 - no impact statements, 1 - at least 1 impact statement)	1	1	1	1	0	0	1	1	1	1	1	1	1	1	1	1	1	1	0	1	0	1	1	1	1	1	1	1	0
TOTAL (Executive Review + Legislative Review + Economic Impact)	30	16	16	0	21	13	23	22	10	24	15	24	15	10	21	19	19	17	7	12	27	19	27	15	16	22	11	14	14

Notes

NOTES TO CHAPTER 1

1. 5 U.S.C. 701–706.
2. Some other scholars such as James Buchanan and Gordon Tullock (1965) use "public choice" theory to refer to government bureaucrats issuing regulations as part of their pursuit of self interest.
3. See also Shesple (1992).
4. U.S. Supreme Court 462 U.S. 919 (1983).
5. 5 U.S.C. 801–808.
6. Executive Order 12866 requires agencies to perform a Regulatory Impact Analysis (RIA) on all regulations with an economic impact of more than $100 million in any year.
7. See http://www.progressivereform.org/CPRBlog.cfm?idBlog=D913A772-BA B5–697D-6638AEC1CF3053DB (last viewed February 18, 2013).

NOTES TO CHAPTER 2

1. 5 U.S.C. 701–706.
2. H.R. 10.
3. H.R. 3010.
4. See the annual reports from the Small Business Administration on the Regulatory Flexibility Act: http://www.sba.gov/advocacy/823/4798 (last viewed February 18, 2013).
5. Indeed, rulemaking output at the federal level tends to increase in Democratic administrations and decrease in Republican administrations (http://cei.org/sites/default/files/Wayne%20Crews%20-%2010,000%20 Commandments%202011.pdf page 39 last viewed January 24, 2012). This has so far not held for the Obama Administration. Rulemaking output also increases in the last year of an administration, when agencies tend to promulgate costly rules (Beerman 2009).
6. As we will discuss in Chapter Five, perceptions about the number of regulations are a key component of the opposition to regulation among business owners.
7. Data was collected from twenty-eight states for which regulations were available online at the time: Arizona, Arkansas, Delaware, Idaho, Illinois, Indiana, Iowa, Kansas, Louisiana, Maine, Michigan, Minnesota, Missouri, Montana, Nevada, New Hampshire, New Jersey, New Mexico, New York, North Carolina, Oklahoma, Pennsylvania, South Dakota, Tennessee, Virginia, Washington, Wisconsin, and Wyoming.

8. A natural question is whether states that put their rules online differ in some meaningful way from states that do not. As described below, we could not find any meaningful differences between states in our sample and states not in it.
9. One possible difficulty is the existing regulatory base in the states. Some states may issue more regulations because they have issued fewer regulations in the past and are merely "catching up" with their peers. While we do not think this is the case, it is extremely difficult to test and therefore to rule out.
10. Because each state requires a public comment period, there was little data to collect on this aspect of rulemaking. We did collect data on whether states require agencies to respond to comment but, as described below, found no significant relationship between that requirement and regulatory output.
11. All states require public comment, so there is no variation in this requirement, which makes it impossible to use as an independent variable. How well states respond to comments may vary, but collecting that data for this volume of regulations is impossible.
12. Of the six states that saw party shifts in the legislative chambers, Indiana, Michigan, Oklahoma, and Wisconsin went from Republican control in 2006 to split partisan leadership of the chambers in 2007; Iowa and Minnesota went from Democratic control in 2006 to split control in 2007.
13. Using a one-sided t-test.
14. The states are Idaho, Indiana, Louisiana, Michigan, Minnesota, and Pennsylvania.
15. While the direction was the same for each policy area, the relationship was statistically significant for transportation regulation and insurance/banking regulation only.
16. The three states are Arizona, New Mexico, and Delaware.
17. These two states are Tennessee and Illinois.
18. Delaware, New Mexico, and Wyoming have no economic analysis of regulations.
19. New York, Virginia, Michigan, and Pennsylvania all received scores of ten.
20. This relationship is also statistically significant for insurance/banking, education, and transportation. States with deadlines and stringent executive review also produce fewer environmental and agriculture regulations than states with deadlines and lax review, but the relationship is not statistically significant.
21. We also tested control of the executive and legislative branches in combination. We found no statistically significant results of interest, including no difference between divided government and unified government.
22. For education, the difference between the last row of the table and the other rows is significant at the 5 percent level using a one-sided t-test. For insurance/banking, it is significant at the 10 percent level.

NOTES TO CHAPTER 3

1. The Worker and Community Right to Know Act (S-1670) was enacted into law in August 1983. An interview with the bill's sponsor, former State Senator Daniel J. Dalton, provided the legislative history and the background on the regulatory implementation that followed.
2. The law, known as EDECA, the Electric Discount and Energy Competition Act, was enacted in 1999 and was envisioned "to produce a wider selection of services at competitive market-based prices."
3. The statute stipulated that the BPU should report back to the legislature on its implementation within three years of the date of enactment; one stakeholder

interviewed indicated it took this long for the Board to adopt many of its regulations.

4. This phrasing was excerpted from Governor Christine Todd Whitman's press release, issued on the day she signed the bill into law.

5. As one marketer whom we interviewed explained, "the market was doomed from the start as the BPU was directed by the legislature to set temporary rate caps for the first few years of the program. In the end, there was more politics than economics in the rates set by the Board. In fact, the utilities were later able to recover 'deferred costs' which amounted to the actual costs of delivering electricity to customers which proved the Board had set the rate caps under the true costs at the time."

6. Market estimates were presented by the New Jersey Ratepayer Advocate at a legislative hearing in March 2001.

7. The viability of the green market was negatively portrayed by a former energy supplier whose company has since left the market.

8. See New Jersey Regulatory Flexibility Act of 1986, Pub. L. No.1986, NJ Laws ch.169, C. 52:14B-19; Pub. L. No.1995, NJ Laws ch.65, C. 52:14B-22–24; Pub. L. No.1995, NJ Laws ch.166, C. 52:14B-4(a) (2); and Pub. L. No.1998, NJ Laws ch.48, C. 52:14B-4(a) (2); see also 4:1C-10.3.

9. P.L. No. 2001, NJ Laws ch.5, C. 52:14B-4(a) (3), 52:14B-4(g) and 52:14B-4(f).

10. N.J. Exec. Order No. 97 (August 2, 1993) directed the Chief Counsel to conduct a comprehensive review of the State's regulatory system and to identify recommendations designed to maximize efficiency, eliminate duplicative and inconsistent regulations, and provide the greatest degree of effective public participation in the rulemaking process. Similarly, N.J. Exec. Order No. 27 (November 2, 1994) ordered State administrative agencies to include a statement whether Federal standards are exceeded when adopting, amending, or readopting regulations.

11. The requirement to add "a description of the expected socio-economic impact of the regulation" was enacted in 1981; see Pub. L. No.1981, NJ Laws ch.27.

12. The General Assembly of the State of NJ v. Byrne, 90 N.J.S.Ct. 376; 448 A.2d 438; 1982 N.J. LEXIS 2165.

13. An agency must publish a quarterly notice of proposed rulemaking activities for the ensuing six-month period. If a calendar is amended, an agency may take no action prior to forty-five days of the published revision to schedule. Exceptions to the calendar requirement include state and federal statutory authorization, imminent peril, a regulation for which a notice of preproposal has been published, or for a regulation proposal that includes a comment period of at least sixty days (OAL Rulemaking Manual, 16–18).

14. Agencies must grant the petition, deny the petition, or refer the petition for further deliberation within defined deadlines.

15. Thad Kousser (2005) has developed a ten-point index to measure professionalism, according to which New Jersey is ranked above the median.

16. The states with legislative veto power that do not require the concurrence of the governor are: Colorado, Connecticut, Georgia, Idaho, Illinoi, Iowa, Kentucky, Louisiana, Nevada, New Jersey, North Dakota, Oklahoma, South Dakota Tennessee, Utah, and West Virginia (Source: Institute for Policy Integrity).

17. We measure controversy by the number of comments received.

18. Each observation is identified by the Proposal Notice New Jersey Register (NJR) Citation, which is assigned by the OAL. The NJR Citation is the Register page number where that proposal was published.

19. A regulation adoption is defined by the OAL Rulemaking Manual; however, for our purposes, an electronic regulation adoption that included more than

one type of regulatory activity was coded as "mixed" (e.g., repeal of a regulation, new regulation proposal, and amendment to an existing regulation) and an activity that did not substantively or permanently impact a proposed regulation or adopted regulation was recorded as "other" (includes waiver of sunset provisions, executive orders, public notices, etc.). In all, ten types of regulation adoptions were identified.

20. Twenty-four agencies were identified. In addition to cabinet-level departments, independent agencies and commissions were recorded separately. Most authorities were categorized together with the exception of the Casino Control Commission (CCC), which generates significant regulatory activity due to the regulated gambling industry housed in Atlantic City, and the Higher Education Commission (HEC), the Election Law Enforcement Commission (ELEC), and the Office of Administrative Law (OAL). A dual department regulatory submission was recorded as "joint"; however, there were limited activities of this kind.

21. If the full text of the proposal was included, the observation was coded as 1. A readopted regulation, without change, is not required to include the full text of the regulation. This distinction was made in order to measure the significance of a regulation as measured by page length.

22. Page length of regulation was calculated based upon the electronic version of the New Jersey Register.

23. Two variables were coded; if comments were received, the observation was coded as 1. The second variable measured the total number of comments received per regulation adoption. Neither variable captured oral or written testimony presented at a public hearing to avoid duplication by individuals.

24. Note: Not all attendees provided testimony, either written or oral, into the record.

25. Total public participation was calculated as the sum of all individual public comments received and the total number of attendees if a public hearing was held. To the extent practical, if a participant testified at a public hearing and submitted written comments during the formal comment period, the latter was not counted in the total of written comments received.

26. A "Summary of Public Comments and Agency Responses" is required as part of the notice of adoption process. According to the OAL Rulemaking Manual, such response may take the form of a "Summary of Agency Initiated Changes," a "Summary of Changes Upon Adoption," and/or a "Response to a Comment." Controlling for duplications, if any of these change were included in a regulation adoption, the observation was coded as 1.

27. The regulatory adoption activity excluded represents less than .02 percent of the total public participation received over the study period. Of the total 936 regulations that received comments in the full model, only forty-four regulations were excluded.

28. On average, 535 regulations were proposed and 565 adopted (1998–2002) compared to 524 proposed and 535 adopted (2003–2007).

29. A reproposal may be in response to issued raised by commenters or changes generated after further staff review. The notice of reproposal must reflect, "to a significant degree", the original notice of proposal. (See OAL Rulemaking Manual, 45).

30. Similar observations were offered by public officials involved in the Pennsylvania rulemaking process that we interviewed in Chapter Seven.

31. Language as contained in N.J.A.C. 1:30–6.3.

32. This mirrors an approach used by interest groups in Pennsylvania described in Chapter Seven.

33. N.J. Register Vol. 30 No. 3, Division of Consumer Affairs, Orthotics and Prosthetics Board of Examiners, "Regulations of Practice" (February 2, 1998).

N.J. Register Vol. 30 No. 13, State Board of Education, "Special Education" (July 6, 1998). N.J. Register Vol. 30 No. 11, Division of Motor Vehicles, "Standards For Motor Vehicles With Elevated Chassis Height" (June 1, 1998).

34. Twenty one states have placed deadlines on an agency's rulemaking calendar) (see Table 3 in Appendix for list of states with deadlines); however, there is wide variation in the time limits set by states. Six states also set a minimum time on an agency before it can adopt a regulation following its proposal or public comment period (Alabama, Idaho, Louisiana, Maryland, Michigan, and Utah).

35. N.J. Register Vol. 38 No. 23, Department of Environmental Protection, "Highlands Water Protection and Planning Act Regulations" (December 4, 2006).

36. N.J. Register Volume 38 No. 10, Department of Environmental Protection, "Horseshoe Crabs" (May 15, 2006).

37. N.J. Register Volume 31 No. 8, Department of Corrections, "Deposits And Deductions Commissary" (April 19, 1999).

38. N.J. Register Volume 31 No. 5, Department of Human Services, "Long Term Care Services Manual" (March 1, 1999).

39. N.J. Register Volume 31 No. 19, Department of Transportation, "Truck Access" (October 4, 1999).

40. If the intention of these impact statements is to lessen the economic burden on regulated entities, it is hard to argue from this data that they have had such an effect.

41. Our analysis of legislative review in New Jersey extended from 1996 to 2011, the period for which archived records of legislative sessions are readily available to the public. Legislative review became effective on December 3, 1992.

NOTES TO CHAPTER 4

1. A report by the Institute for Policy Integrity (Livermore Piennar and Schwartz 2012) found a 17,550 percent increase in the use of the term "job-killing regulations" between 2007 and 2011 in U.S. newspapers.

2. The debate continues. As we went to press, competing analyses of the impact of regulations on employment were issued by the Chamber of Commerce (which said there was a negative impact) and by the Environmental Protection Agency (which said that there wasn't) (Goad 2013).

3. Representative Jeb Hensarling (R-Tex) justified the Republican regulatory reform bill, the REINS Act, by saying, "It simply weighs the benefits of a regulation to be balanced with the cost to our own jobs. Jobs ought to be number one in this House, and the number one jobs bill we can pass is the REINS Act." See: (Sonmez 2013).

4. Indeed, as shown in Chapter Three (NJ case study) and Chapter Five, for the five states for which we collected data on multiple years, the same states regularly promulgated more regulations.

NOTES TO CHAPTER 5

1. See http://mittromneycentral.com/on-the-issues/limited-government/ (last accessed February 2013).

2. See http://mittromneycentral.com/speeches/2012-speeches/102612-remarks-on-the-american-economy/ (last accessed February 2013).

3. We would have included Iowa and Ohio in our design; however, data was not available online for all years specified within the longitudinal design.

4. See http://walker.wi.gov/Default.aspx?Page=b5a8a449–5df3–49fa-af83–6eb
   2e3fdbb86 (last accessed May 4, 2013).
5. In a recent *New York Times* article, Governor Snyder has been described
   as a political enigma who defies political labels. (Of note, Snyder currently
   occupies an office that regularly faces partisan turnovers.) NYT article
   last accessed May 2, 2013 at http://msue.anr.msu.edu/news/department_
   of_insurance_and_financial_services_protects_consumers.
6. See http://www.michigan.gov/som/0,4669,7–192–29701–293041—,00.html
   (last accessed May 4, 2013).
7. Dayton is a member of the Minnesota Democratic-Farmer-Labor Party,
   which affiliates nationally with the Democratic Party.
8. See http://radiooneindiana.com/index.php/region-news/944-governor-pences-
   1st-state-of-the-state-address.html (last accessed May 4, 2013).
9. To be fair, the moratorium imposed by Governor Pence is different than the
   other measures discussed here. As long as the moratorium is in place, there
   will be no new regulations in Indiana. However, it does nothing to address
   the existing stock of regulations that, according to the rhetoric, are the source
   of the problem.
10. Governor Walker proclaimed the following in his 2013 State of the State
    address: "In a survey, we asked employers what we can do to help them cre-
    ate jobs in the upcoming year and the most common answer was decrease the
    amount of state regulations." *Supra* Footnote 4.
11. See U.S. Bureau of Labor Statistics (2007) Local Area Unemployment Statistics.
    Available online at http://www.bls.gov/lau/lastrk07.htm (last accessed October
    2011).
12. Wisconsin does not impose a procedural deadline on rulemaking from the
    time of proposal to adoption.
13. Such was the case of EDECA in the NJ case study, as described by one mar-
    keter we interviewed. See Chapter 3.
14. See U.S. Census Bureau, various state Quick Fact Sheets.
15. See U.S. Census Bureau (2007) Statistics of U.S. Businesses (SUSB) Data.
    Available online at: http://www.census.gov/econ/susb/data/susb2007.html
    (last accessed October 2011).
16. See Borie-Holtz, Van Horn, and Zukin (2010).
17. Results for the total dataset are based on telephone interviews with 604
    small-business owners, conducted Oct. 3–6, 2011. For results based on the
    total sample of small-business owners, one can say with 95 percent confi-
    dence that the maximum margin of sampling error is ±4 percentage points.
    Sampling is done on an Random Digit Dialing basis using Dun & Bradstreet
    sampling of small businesses having $20 million or less of sales or revenues.
    The data is weighted to be representative of U.S. small businesses within this
    size range nationwide.
18. Nonprofit organization make up a small percent, but we wanted to include
    them since they operate as members of a regulated community.
19. When the weights were applied, there was no statistical mean difference
    between the weighted and unweighted samples; the weighted mean differ-
    ence was 55 percent.
20. The telephone and abbreviated email instrument only asked two open-ended
    questions of all respondents. The results reported above in Table 5.5 include
    all modes. There were no differences in terms of low identification rates or
    the state-specific measures offered by respondents due to mode. All respon-
    dents were hard-pressed to single out a state law or regulation impacting
    their business operations.
21. The perception that regulations have a negative impact on businesses was a
    consistent theme presented in a recent Pennsylvania state legislative hearing

held in March 2013. Similarly, when industry representatives were probed for examples by members of the committee, few if any were offered. This pending legislative debate is discussed further in Chapter Seven.

22. When you allow for regression to the mean, this enthusiasm for the future may be even more dismal given the skewed distribution of how business executives view the past (74 percent hold a negative view of the past five years).

23. While we do not know the general population parameters for party affiliation for business executives, it is not unrealistic to expect to find more Republicans than Democrats in the sample. This is also one of the reasons we include party identification among the demographics, as we hypothesize it helps explain some of the political rhetoric.

24. Seventy-eight percent of survey respondents say they can "live with some regulation but there is too much now in the economy."

NOTES TO CHAPTER 6

1. The average score for the legislative review and executive review variables was five and for the analysis variable was a six. This differs only slightly (and not significantly) from the averages for the twenty-eight states used in Chapter Two.

2. These scales are available at www.unc.edu/~beyle/gubnewpwr.html (last viewed February 27, 2013).

3. See http://www.bama.ua.edu/~rcfording/readme_update2010.pdf.

4. Citizen ideology was removed from the model because it was highly colinear with legislative party control. Including it in lieu of legislative party control did not substantially change the results of the regression.

5. See http://walker.wi.gov/Default.aspx?Page=b5a8a449-5df3-49fa-af83-6eb 2e3fdbb86 Last viewed May 4, 2013.

6. Rosenthal did a survey of state legislators in five states and the legislators rated constituent service as a 4.46 out of five on a scale of the importance of their various tasks. (p. 29)

7. The negative relationship between professionalism and legislative review bears comment. The most likely explanation is that less professional legislatures are in session less and hence are more likely to need a meaningful legislative review process to intervene in agency decisions.

NOTES TO CHAPTER 7

1. See Appendix 4 for the full rankings of the fifty states for executive and legislative review as well as economic analysis.

2. 732–204(b)(i 1–3).

3. 732–204 (c).

4. 71 P.S. §§ 745.1–745.15.

5. In the 1982 Act, the IRRC was given authority to review only proposed rules. In a 1989 revision of the Act (P.L.73, No.19), the IRRC was required to review both proposed and final rules.

6. P.L.277, No.60.

7. P.L.657, No.76.

8. In an interview with representatives in the Office of General Council in the Corbin Administration, attorneys generally acknowledged that reviews were conducted on a first-in, first-out basis; the review time frame often depended upon the number of rules received and when they were received. A typical review could take three weeks, but generally not more than two months.

9. P.L.73, No.19.
10. *Department of Environmental Resources v. Jubelier* 567 A.2d 741 (PA Commw. Ct. 1989).
11. The number of regulations reviewed by the IRRC has gone down over the years. However, because data is scarce before the creation of the IRRC, it is difficult to ascribe this reduction to the presence of the IRRC. It is certainly possible that the decreased number of rules is due to the IRRC and the deadlines on rulemaking (which we saw were important in Chapter Two), but in an individual case, determining causality is impossible.
12. The Department of Environmental Resources, which was split into the Department of Environmental Protection and the Department of Conservation and Natural Resources in the 1990s.
13. These requirements were strengthened in 2011. Unfortunately, no current legislators agreed to speak with us.
14. Op. Cit. Shawn Good from the Pennsylvania Chamber of Business and Industry, offered these remarks in his summary of how the pending legislation would improve the current process.
15. Comments are taken from written testimony presented into the public record by Cara Sullivan, Director of the Commerce, Insurance, and Economic Development Task Force at ALEC. ALEC is a self-reported non-profit think tank for state-based public policy issues focused on the principles of free markets, limited government, and the constitutional division of powers between the federal and state governments.
16. In written testimony presented by Shawn Good on behalf of the Pennsylvania Chamber of Business & Industry to the House State Government Committee on March 19, 2013, Good wrote: ". . . I would like to be clear that under the current regulatory review process, the Pennsylvania Chamber and its members have long-standing working relationships with the regulatory agencies, and these relationships are of great benefit to our overall, broad-based membership." Good cited two examples in which the chamber worked with agencies during the rulemaking process. In one procedural matter, the focus of the rule proposal was to provide greater predictability and certainty during the review of environmental permits; in another case, he described how the Chamber worked to remove certain proposed provisions that would have had a negative economic impact on some industries in the state.
17. All oral comments presented at the hearing were excerpted from a transcript compiled by a legislative monitoring service, which summarized the House State Government Committee hearing held on March 19, 2013. In an exchange between Cara Sullivan and a committee member, Rep. Brian Sims (D) asked Sullivan if "she could point to any Pennsylvania regulations that are unnecessary or unfair. Sullivan replied, 'Unfortunately, I am not an expert on Pennsylvania regulations.'" Another expert who testified at the hearing described a federal regulatory process that incentivized federal bureaucrats to promulgate rules and added that "is probably true at the state level as well."
18. One of the coauthors testified at this hearing while this book was under review.
19. Oral comments were again excerpted from a transcript compiled by a legislative monitoring service, which provided a summary of the House State Government Committee hearing held on April 24, 2013.
20. One exception to this may be the deadline for completing rules, which several interview subjects mentioned as difficult to meet (particularly with all of the layers of review that a rule must go through).
21. SB 250 was passed over the veto of Governor Hunt.
22. 304 N.C. 591 286 S.E. 2d 79 (1982).
23. See for example S.L. 1989–5, S.L. 1991–418, S.L. 1991–477, S.L. 2003–229.

24. This committee was renamed the Regulatory Reform Committee in 2011.
25. The requirement for legislative review required agencies to delay the effectiveness of the rule until after the next legislative session following its issuance. This led to numerous conflicts, with statutes passed requiring rules by a certain date. Agencies responded by promulgating temporary regulations, which were exempt from the legislative review provision. The proliferation of temporary rules led the legislature to revise the procedure in 2003, subjecting only rules that received more than 10 comments to legislative review.
26. See http://pulse.ncpolicywatch.org/2011/06/30/nc-environmentalists-applaud-governors-vetoes/ (last viewed January 14, 2013).
27. See also Rossi (2001).
28. This could be due to the fact that the governor's mansion has often been controlled by the same party as the legislature (until recently, the Democrats have had unified control).
29. For example, the new head of the North Carolina Department of Environment and Natural Resources is a former legislature whose office window faced the Department and who drew a target on his window. See: http://projects.newsobserver.com/under_the_dome/rep_gillespie_leaving_house_to_join_denr_an_agency_he_targeted (last viewed February 22, 2013).

NOTES TO CHAPTER 8

1. Business owners in North Carolina cited local ordinances more often that state regulations when pressed for specific examples of burdensome regulations according to this individual.
2. In fact, the federal Congressional Review Act has been used a grand total of one time to repeal an executive branch regulation (Finkel and Sullivan 2011). In Chapter Three we detailed how legislative review in New Jersey has resulted in the repeal of zero regulations in the twenty years it has been in effect.
3. In Rhode Island, Governor Lincoln Chafee required all state agencies to expedite a review of all existing regulations for harmful impacts on small businesses (n = 1,638). He ordered members of his cabinet and agency heads to accelerate the review and complete 25 percent by Dec. 31, 2012 and another 25 percent every four months until completed. By the calendar, 50 percent should have been completed by April, 2013; however, a status of the review was not available at the time of publication. At the federal level, President Obama's review of regulations has been criticized as producing one or two significant changes but not much else.

Bibliography

Ackerman, Frank, and Lisa Heinzerling. *Priceless: On Knowing the Price of Everything and the Value of Nothing.* New York: The New Press, 2004.

Arbuckle, Donald. "The Role of Analysis on the 17 Most Political Acres on the Face of the Earth." *Risk Analysis* 31 (2011): 884–892.

Arora, Seema, and Timothy Cason. "Why Do Firms Volunteer to Exceed Environmental Regulations? Understanding Participation in EPA's 33/50 Program." *Land Economics* 72 (1996): 413–32.

Balla, Steven. "Administrative Procedures and Political Control of the Bureaucracy." *American Political Science Review* 92 (1998): 663–73.

———. "Legislative Organization and Congressional Review of Agency Regulations." *Journal of Law, Economics, and Organization* 16 (2000a): 424–448.

———. "Political and Organizational Determinants of Bureaucratic Responsiveness." *American Politics Quarterly* 28 (2000b): 163–193.

Ballantine, Patrick. "Common Sense Reform: A Legislator's Viewpoint." *Wake Forest Law Review* 31 (1996): 799–807.

Becker, Gary. "A Theory of Competition Among Pressure Groups for Political Influence." *Quarterly Journal of Economics* 98 (1983): 371–400.

Becker, Randy A., and J. Vernon Henderson. "Costs of Air Quality Regulation." In *Behavioral and Distributional Effects of Environmental Policy,* edited by Carlo Carraro and Gilbert E. Metcalf, 159–86. Chicago: University of Chicago Press, 2009.

Beermann, Jack. "Combating Midnight Regulation." *Northwestern University Law Review* 103 (2009): 352–69.

Berman, Eli, and Linda T. M. Bui. "Environmental Regulation and Labor Demand: Evidence from the South Coast Air Basin." *Journal of Public Economics* 79 (2001a): 265–95.

———. "Environmental Regulation and Productivity: Evidence from Oil Refineries." *The Review of Economics and Statistics* 83 (2001b): 498–510.

Berry, William D., Evan J. Ringquist, Richard C. Fording, and Russell L. Hanson. "Measuring Citizen and Government Ideology in the American States, 1960–93." *American Journal of Political Science* 42 (1998): 327–48.

Beyle, Thad L. "Enhancing Executive Leadership in the States." *State and Local Government Review* 27 (1995): 18–35.

Blumstein, James F. "Presidential Administration and Administrative Law: Regulatory Review by the Executive Office of The President: An Overview and Policy Analysis of Current Issues." *Duke Law Journal* 51 (2001): 851–99.

Borie-Holtz, Debra, Carl Van Horn, and Cliff Zukin. "No End in Sight: The Agony of Prolonged Unemployment." Paper presented at American Association for Public Opinion Research (AAPOR) Annual Conference, Chicago, November 2010.

Buchanan, James and Gordon Tullock. *The Calculus of Consent: Logical Foundations of Constitutional Democracy.* Ann Arbor, MI: University of Michigan Press, 1965.

Calvert, Randall L., and Barry R. Weingast. "Runaway Bureaucracy and Congressional Oversight: Why Reforms Fail." *Review of Policy Research* 1 (1982): 557–64.

Card, David, and Alan B. Krueger. *Myth and Measurement: The New Economics of the Minimum Wage.* Princeton, NJ: Princeton University Press, 1997.

Carrigan, Christopher, and Cary Coglianese. "The Politics of Regulation: From New Institutionalism to New Governance." *Annual Review of Political Science* 14 (2011): 107–29.

Clingermayer, James C., and William F. West. "Imposing Procedural Constraints on State Administrative Agencies: An Empirical Investigation of Competing Explanations." *Review of Policy Research* 11 (1992): 37–56.

Coglianese, Cary. "Assessing Consensus: The Promise and Performance of Negotiated Rulemaking." *Duke Law Journal* 46 (1997): 1255–349.

———. "Empirical Analysis and Administrative Law." *University of Illinois Law Review* 2002 (2002): 1111–38.

———. "Has Judicial Review Caused a Rulemaking Retreat?" Paper presented at The Law and Society conference, Denver, CO, May 2009.

———. "Regulation and Unemployment" Wharton Public Policy Initiative Issue Brief, 2013 (available at: https://publicpolicy.wharton.upenn.edu/files/2013/04/PPI-issue-brief_vol01no03_final-1.pdf).

Copeland, Brian R., and M. Scott Taylor. "North-South Trade and the Environment." *The Quarterly Journal of Economics* 109 (1994): 755–87.

———. "Trade, Growth, and the Environment." *American Economic Association* 42 (2004): 7–71.

Crews, Clyde Wayne. "Ten Thousand Commandments: An Annual Snapshot of the Regulatory State." Editorial. Competitive Enterprise Institute Free Markets and Limited Government, 2012 (available at http://cei.org/sites/default/files/Wayne%20Crews%20-%2010,000%20Commandments%202012_0.pdf).

Croley, Steven P. "Theories of Regulation: Incorporating the Administrative Process." *Columbia Law Review* 98 (1998): 1–168.

———. "White House Review of Agency Rulemaking: An Empirical Investigation." *University of Chicago Law Review* 70 (2003): 821–885.

Cropper, Maureen L., and Wallace E. Oates. "Environmental Economics: A Survey." *Journal of Economic Literature* 30 (1992): 675–740.

Daley, Dorothy M., Donald P. Haider-Markel, and Andrew B. Whitford. "Checks, Balances, and the Cost of Regulation: Evidence from the American States." *Political Research Quarterly* 60, no. 4 (2007): 696–706.

Davis, Kenneth Culp. *Discretionary Justice: A Preliminary Inquiry.* Baton Rouge, LA: Louisiana State University Press, 1969.

Davis, Steven J., and Till M. von Wachter. "Recessions and the Costs of Job Loss." *Brookings Papers on Economic Activity* 43 (2011): 1–72.

DeMuth, Christopher. "OIRA at Thirty." *Administrative Law Review* 63 (2011): 101–11.

Dillman, Donald, Jolene D. Smyth, and Leah Melani Christian. *Internet, Mail and Mixed-Mode Surveys: The Tailored Design Method.* Malden, MA: John Wiley and Sons, Inc.,2008.

Dometrius, Nelson C. "Gubernatorial Approval and Administrative Influence." *State Politics and Policy Quarterly* 2 (2002): 251–67.

Downs, Anthony. *Inside Bureaucracy.* New York: Little Brown, 1967.

Eisner, Marc Allen. *Regulatory Politics in Transition.* Baltimore: Johns Hopkins University Press, 2000.

Elliott, E. Donald. "Re-Inventing Rulemaking." *Duke Law Journal* 41 (1992): 1490–96.

Epstein, David, and Sharyn O'Halloran. *Delegating Powers: A Transaction Cost Politics Approach to Policy Making under Separate Powers.* Cambridge, UK: Cambridge University Press, 1999.

Ethridge, Marcus E. "A Political-Institutional Interpretation of Legislative Oversight Mechanisms and Behavior." *Palgrave Macmillan Journals* 17 (1984): 340–59.

Finkel, Adam M., and Jason W. Sullivan. "A Cost-Benefit Interpretation of the 'Substantially Similar' Hurdle in the Congressional Review Act: Can OSHA Ever Utter the E-Word (Ergonomics) Again?" *Administrative Law Review* 63 (2011): 707–783.

Fiorina, Morris P. *Congress: Keystone of the Washington Establishment.* New Haven, CT: Yale University Press, 1989.

———. "Keystone Reconsidered." In *Congress Reconsidered,* edited by Lawrence C. Dodd and Bruce Ian Oppenheimer. Thousand Oaks, CA: CQ Press, 2008.

———. "Legislative Choice of Regulatory Forms: Legal Process or Administrative Process." *Public Choice* 39 (1982): 33–66.

Fiorina, Morris P., and Roger G. Noll. "Voters, Bureaucrats, and Legislators: A Rational Choice Perspective on the Growth of Bureaucracy." *Journal of Public Economics* 9 (1978a): 239–54.

———. "Voters, Legislators and Bureaucracy: Institutional Design in the Public Sector." *The American Economic Review* 68 (1978b): 256–60.

Gerber, Brian J., Cherie Maestas, and Nelson C. Dometrius. "State Legislative Influence over Agency Rulemaking: The Utility of Ex Ante Review." *State Politics and Policy Quarterly* 5 (2005): 24–46.

Gersen, Jacob E., and Anne Joseph O'Connell. "Deadlines in Administrative Law." *University of Pennsylvania Law Review* 156 (2008): 924–71.

Goad, Ben. "Chamber Study Claims to Debunk EPA Figures on Job-Creating Regulations." *The Hill* (available at http://thehill.com/blogs/regwatch/energyenvironment/285359-chamber-study-claims-to-debunk-epas-job-creation-figures). Last accessed June 17, 2013.

Golden, Marissa Martino. "Interest Groups in the Rule-Making Process: Who Participates? Whose Voices Get Heard?" *Journal of Public Administration* 8 (1998): 245–70.

Grady, Dennis O., and Kathleen M. Simon. "Political Restraints and Bureaucratic Discretion: The Case of State Government Rule Making." *Politics and Policy* 30 (2002): 646–79.

Grossman, Gene M., and Alan B. Krueger. "Environmental Impacts of a North American Free Trade Agreement." In *The U.S. Mexico Free Trade Agreement,* edited by Peter Garber, 13–56. Cambridge, MA: MIT Press, 1994.

Gray, Virginia. "Innovation in the States: A Diffusion Study." *The American Political Science Review* 67 (1973): 1174–85.

Gray, Wayne B., and Ronald J. Shadbegian. "Environmental Regulation, Investment Timing, and Technology Choice." *The Journal of Industrial Economics* 46 (1998): 235–56.

Greenstone, Michael. "The Impacts of Environmental Regulations on Industrial Activity: Evidence from the 1970 and 1977 Clean Air Act Amendments and the Census of Manufactures." *Journal of Political Economy* 110 (2002): 1175–219.

Greenstone, Michael, John A. List, and Chad Syverson. "The Effects of Environmental Regulation on the Competitiveness of U.S. Manufacturing." US Census Bureau Center for Economic Studies Paper No. CES-WP-11-03. February 1, 2011.

Grossman, Gene M., and Alan B. Krueger. *Environmental Impacts of a North American Free Trade Agreement.* No. w3914. National Bureau of Economic Research, 1991.

Gutmann, Amy, and Dennis Thompson. *Why Deliberative Democracy?* Princeton, NJ: Princeton University Press, 2004.

Hahn, Robert W. "Cost Benefit Analysis: Legal, Economic, and Philosophical Perspectives: State and Federal Regulatory Reform: A Comparative Analysis." *Journal of Legal Studies* 29 (2000): 873–912.

Hahn, Robert, Jason K. Burnett, Yee-Ho I. Chan, Elizabeth A. Mader, and Petrea R. Moyle. "Assessing Regulatory Impact Analyses: The Failure of Agencies to

Comply with Executive Order 12,866." *Harvard Journal of Law and Public Policy* 23 (2000): 859–885.

Harter, Philip J. "Assessing the Assessors: The Actual Performance of Regulatory Negotiation." *NYU Environmental Law Journal* 9 (2001) 32–45.

———. "Negotiating Regulations: A Cure for the Malaise?" *Environmental Impact Assessment Review* 3 (1982) 75–91.

Hill, Jeffrey S., and James E. Brazier. "Constraining Administrative Decisions: A Critical Examination of the Structure and Process Hypothesis." *Journal of Law, Economics, and Organization* 7 (1991): 373–400.

Horn, Murray J., and Kenneth A. Shepsle. "Commentary on 'Administrative Arrangements and the Political Control of Agencies': Administrative Process and Organizational Form as Legislative Responses to Agency Costs." *Virginia Law Review* 75 (1989): 499–508.

Huber, John D., and Charles R. Shipan. *Deliberate Discretion?: The Institutional Foundations of Bureaucratic Autonomy.* Cambridge, UK: Cambridge University Press, 2002.

Huber, John D., Charles R. Shipan, and Madelaine Pfahler. "Legislatures and Statutory Control of Bureaucracy." *American Journal of Political Science* 45 (2001): 330–45.

Jaffe, Adam B., Steven R. Peterson, Paul R. Portney, and Robert N. Stavins. "Environmental Regulation and the Competitiveness of U.S. Manufacturing: What Does the Evidence Tell Us?" *Journal of Economic Literature* 33 (1995): 132–63.

Jewell, Malcolm Edwin, and Marcia Lynn Whicker. *Legislative Leadership in the American States.* Ann Arbor, MI: University of Michigan Press, 1994.

Johnson, Stephen M. "The Internet Changes Everything: Revolutionizing Public Participation and Access to Government Information through the Internet." *Administrative Law Review* 50 (1998): 277–82.

———. "Ossification's Demise: An Empirical Analysis of EPA Rulemaking from 2001–2005." *Environmental Law* 38 (2008): 767–792.

Jorgenson, Dale W., and Peter J. Wilcoxen. "The Economic Impact of the Clean Air Act Amendments of 1990." *The Energy Journal* 14 (1993): 159–82.

Kagan, Elena. "Presidential Administration." *Harvard Law Review* 114 (2001): 2245–385.

Katzen, Sally. "A Reality Check on an Empirical Study: Comments on 'Inside the Administrative State'." *Michigan Law Review* 105 (May 2007): 1497–1510.

Kerwin, Cornelius M., and Scott R. Furlong. "Time and Rulemaking: An Empirical Test of Theory." *Journal of Public Administration Research and Theory* 2 (1992): 113–38.

King, Gary, Robert O. Keohane, and Sidney Verba. *Designing Social Inquiry: Scientific Inference in Qualitative Research.* Princeton, NJ: Princeton University Press, 1994.

Kousser, Thad. *Term Limits and the Dismantling of State Legislative Professionalism.* Cambridge, UK: Cambridge University Press, 2005.

Krause, George A. "Federal Reserve Policy Decision Making: Political and Bureaucratic Influences." *American Journal of Political Science* 38 (1994): 124–144.

Levin, Ronald M. "Modernizing Agency Practice: The 2010 Model State Administrative Procedure Act." *Widener Law Journal* 20 (2011): 707–855.

Levine, Michael E. "Regulation, the Market, and Interest Group Cohesion: Why Airlines Were Not Reregulated." In *Creating Competitive Markets: The Politics of Regulatory Reform,* edited by Marc Karnis Landy. Washington, DC: Brookings Institution Press, 2007.

Livermore, Michael A., Elizabeth Piennar, and Jason A. Schwartz. "The Regulatory Red Herring: The Role of Job Impact Analysis in Environmental Policy Debates." Institute for Policy Integrity, New York University School of Law, April 2012.

Low, Patrick, and Alexander Yeats. "Do 'Dirty' Industries Migrate?" in *International Trade and the Environment*. Washington, DC: The World Bank, 1992.

Lupia, Arthur, and Mathew D. McCubbins. "Designing Bureaucratic Accountability." *Law and Contemporary Problems* 57 (1994) 91–126.

Mashaw, Jerry L. and David L. Harfst. *The Struggle for Auto Safety.* Cambridge, MA: Harvard University Press, 1990.

Masur, Jonathan S., and Eric A. Posner. "Regulation, Unemployment, and Cost-Benefit Analysis." *Virginia Law Review* 98 (2012) 579–680.

Mayhew, David R. *Congress: The Electoral Connection.* New Haven, CT: Yale University Press, 2004.

Meyer, Stephen M. *Environmentalism and Economic Prosperity: Testing the Environmental Impact Hypothesis.* Cambridge, MA: M.I.T. Project on Environmental Politics and Policy, 1992.

McCubbins, Mathew D., Roger G. Noll, and Barry R. Weingast. "Administrative Procedures as Instruments of Political Control." *Journal of Law, Economics, and Organization* 3 (1987): 243–77.

———. "Structure and Process, Politics and Policy: Administrative Arrangements and the Political Control of Agencies." *Virginia Law Review* 75 (1989): 431–82.

McCubbins, Mathew D., and Thomas Schwartz. "Congressional Oversight Overlooked: Police Patrols versus Fire Alarms." *American Journal of Political Science* 28 (1984): 165–79.

McGarity, Thomas O. "Some Thoughts on 'Deossifying' the Rulemaking Process." *Duke Law Journal* 41 (1992): 1385–462.

McGuire, Martin C. "Regulation, Factor Rewards, and International Trade." *Journal of Public Economics* 17 (1982): 335–54.

Mendelson, Nina A. "Rulemaking, Democracy, and Torrents of E-Mail." *George Washington Law Review* 79 (2011): 1343–1381.

Mitchell, Charlotte A. "The North Carolina Rules Review Commission: A Constitutional Quandary." *North Carolina Law Review* 82 (2004): 2092–2127.

Moe, Terry M. "An Assessment of the Positive Theory of 'Congressional Dominance.' " *Legislative Studies Quarterly* 12 (1987): 475–520.

———. "Political Institutions: The Neglected Side of the Story." *Journal of Law, Economics, and Organization* 6 (1990): 213–53.

Morgenstern, Richard D., William A. Pizer, and Jhih-Shyang Shih. "Jobs versus the Environment: An Industry-Level Perspective." *Journal of Environmental Economics and Management* 43 (2002): 412–36.

Morrison, Alan B. "OMB Interference with Agency Rulemaking: The Wrong Way to Write a Regulation." *Harvard Law Review* 99 (1986): 1059–74.

Mutz, Diana. *Population-Based Survey Experiments.* Princeton, NJ: Princeton University Press, 2011.

Nathan, Richard P. *The Administrative Presidency.* Hoboken, NJ: Wiley, 1983.

Nichols, Jackson. "The New North Carolina APA: A Practical Guide to Understanding and Using It." *Campbell Law Review* 9 (1987): 293–346.

Niskanen, William A. *Bureaucracy and Representative Government.* Chicago: Aldine-Atherton, 1971.

O'Connell, Anne Joseph. "Political Cycles of Rulemaking: An Empirical Portrait of the Modern Administrative State." *Virginia Law Review* 94 (2008): 889–986.

"Oversight and Insight: Legislative Review of Agencies and Lessons from the States." *Harvard Law Review* 121 (2007): 613–35.

Peltzman, Sam. "Toward a More General Theory of Regulation." *Journal of Law and Economics* 19 (1976): 211–40.

Pethig, Rüdiger. "Environmental Management in General Equilibrium: A New Incentive Compatible Approach." *International Economic Review* 20 (1979): 1–27.

Porter, Michael E. *Competitive Advantage of Nations.* New York: Free Press, 1998.

Porter, Michael E., and Claas van der Linde. "Green and Competitive: Ending the Stalemate." *Harvard Business Review* 73 (1995) 120–134.

Portney, Paul. "The Benefits and Costs of Regulatory Analysis." In *Environmental Policy under Reagan's Executive Order: The Role of Benefit-Cost Analysis,* edited by V. Kerry Smith, 226–40. Chapel Hill, NC: University Of North Carolina Press, 1984.

Power, Robert C. "Rulemaking Developments." *Widener Journal of Public Law* 8 (1999): 419–455.

Quiroga, Miguel, Thomas Sterner, and Martin Persson. "Have Countries with Lax Environmental Regulations a Comparative Advantage in Polluting Industries?" *Working Papers in Economics,* 2009.

Reich, Robert B. "Public Administration and Public Deliberation: An Interpretive Essay." *The Yale Law Journal* 94 (1985): 1617–41.

Rosenthal, Alan. *Heavy Lifting: The Job of the American Legislature.* Washington, DC: CQ Press, 2004.

Rosenthal, Alan, John Hibbing, Burdett Loomis, and Karl Kurtz. *The Case for Representative Democracy.* Washington, DC: CQ Press, 2002.

Rossi, Jim. "Overcoming Parochialism: State Administrative Procedure and Institutional Design." *Administrative Law Review* 53 (2001) 551–573.

———. "Participation Run Amok: The Costs of Mass Participation for Deliberative Agency Decisionmaking." *Northwestern University Law Review* 92 (1997): 173–205.

Rubin, Herbert J., and Irene Rubin. *Qualitative Interviewing: The Art of Hearing Data.* Thousand Oaks, CA: Sage Publications, 1995.

Rugman, Alan M., and Alain Verbeke. "Corporate Strategies and Environmental Regulations." In *International Business: Multinationals in a Social and Regional Context,* edited by Alan M. Rugman, 285–301. New York: Taylor and Francis, 2002.

Schultz-Bressman, Lisa, and Michael P. Vandenbergh. "Inside the Administrative State: A Critical Look at the Practice of Presidential Control." *Michigan Law Review* 105 (2006) 47–99.

Schwartz, Jason A. *52 Experiments with Regulatory Review: The Political and Economic Inputs into State Rulemaking.* Report no. 6. New York: Institute for Policy Integrity, 2010.

Shapiro, Stuart. "Presidents and Process: A Comparison of the Regulatory Process under the Clinton and Bush (43) Administrations." *Journal of Law and Politics* 23 (2007): 393–418.

———. "Speedbumps and Roadblocks: Procedural Controls and Regulatory Change." *Journal of Public Administration Research and Theory* 12 (2002): 29–58.

———. "Unequal Partners: Cost-Benefit Analysis and Executive Review of Regulations." *The Environmental Law Reporter* 35 (2005): 10433–44.

Shapiro, Stuart, and John F. Morrall III. "The Triumph of Regulatory Politics: Benefit Cost Analysis and Political Salience." *Regulation and Governance* 6 (2012): 189–206.

Shepsle, Kenneth A. "Bureaucratic drift, coalitional drift, and time consistency: A comment on Macey." *Journal of Law, Economics, & Organization* 8, no. 1 (1992): 111–118.

Shipan, Charles R., and Craig Volden. "The Mechanisms of Policy Diffusion." *American Journal of Political Science* 52 (2008): 840–57.

Siebert, Horst. "Environmental Quality and the Gains from Trade." *Kyklos* 30 (1977): 657–73.

Sinclair, Tara, and Kathryn Vesey. "Regulation, Jobs, and Economic Growth: An Empirical Analysis" working paper George Washington University Regulatory

Studies Center, 2012 (available at: http://research.columbian.gwu.edu/regulatorystudies/sites/default/files/u41/032212_sinclair_vesey_reg_jobs_growth.pdf).

Sonmez, Felicia. "REINS bill to expand Congressional power over executive regulation passed by House." *Washington Post* (available at http://www.washingtonpost.com/blogs/2chambers/post/reins-bill-to-expand-congressional-power-over-executive-regulations-passed-by-house/2011/12/07/gIQAs6VMdO_blog.html). Last accessed June 17, 2013.

Sorens, Jason, and William Ruger. *Freedom in the 50 States: An Index of Personal and Economic Freedom.* Arlington, VA: Mercatus Center, 2009.

Spence, David. "Agency Policy Making and Political Control: Modeling Away the Delegation Problem." *Journal of Public Administration Research and Theory* 7 (1997): 199–219.

Squire, Peverill. "Career Opportunities and Membership Stability in Legislatures." *Legislative Studies Quarterly* 13 (1988): 65–82.

———. "Legislative Professionalization and Membership Diversity in State Legislatures." *Legislative Studies Quarterly* 17 (1992): 69–79.

Staszewski, Glen. "Political Reasons, Deliberative Democracy, and Administrative Law." *Iowa Law Review* 97 (2012) 849–905.

Stigler, George J. "The Theory of Economic Regulation." *The Bell Journal of Economics and Management Science* 2 (1971): 3–21.

Teske, Paul Eric. *Regulation in the States.* Washington, DC: Brookings Institution Press, 2004.

U.S. Bureau of Labor Statistics. Labor Force Statistics from the Current Population Survey, 2007a (available at http://www.bls.gov/cps/minwage2007.htm). Last accessed October 2011.

U.S. Bureau of Labor Statistics. Local Area Unemployment Statistics, 2007b (available at http://www.bls.gov/lau/lastrk07.htm). Last accessed October 2011.

U.S. Bureau of Labor Statistics. Per Capita Personal Income, 2007c (available at http://www.bea.gov/regional/spi/default.cfm?selTable = SA04&selSeries = ancillary). Last accessed October 2011.

U.S. Census Bureau. State Median Income Data, 2007 (available at http://www.census.gov/hhes/www/income/data/statemedian/index.html). Last accessed October 2011.

U.S. Census Bureau. Statistics of U.S. Businesses (SUSB) Data, 2007 (available at http://www.census.gov/econ/susb/data/susb2007.html). Last accessed October 2011.

U.S. Department of Commerce Bureau of Economic Analysis. Gross Domestic Product, 2007 (available at http://www.bea.gov/regional/gsp). Last accessed October 2011.

Vladeck, David, and Thomas McGarity. "Paralysis by Analysis: How Conservatives Plan to Kill Popular Regulation." *American Prospect* (1995).

Volden, Craig. "Delegating Power to Bureaucracies: Evidence from the States." *Journal of Law Economics and Organization* 18 (2002): 187–220.

Wagner, Wendy E. "The CAIR RIA: Advocacy Dressed up as Policy Analysis in Reforming Regulatory Impact Analysis." In *Reforming Regulatory Impact Analysis,* edited by Winston Harrington, Lisa Heinzerling, and Richard Morgenstern, 56–82. New York: Routledge, 2012.

Walker, Jack L. "The Diffusion of Innovations among the American States." *The American Political Science Review* 63 (1969): 880–99.

Walker, Reed. "The Transitional Costs of Sectoral Reallocation: Evidence from the Clean Air Act and the Workforce." US Census Bureau Center for Economic Studies Paper No. CES-WP- 12–02, 2012.

Walley, Noah, and Bradley Whitehead. "It's Not Easy Being Green." *Harvard Business Review* 72 (1994): 46–52.

West, William F. "Formal Procedures, Informal Processes, Accountability, and Responsiveness in Bureaucratic Policy Making: An Institutional Policy Analysis." *Public Administration Review* 64 (2004): 66–80.

———. "Inside the Black Box: The Development of Proposed Rules and the Limits of Procedural Controls." *Administration and Society* 41 (2009): 576–99.

Whisnant, Richard, and Diane DeWitt Cherry. "Economic Analysis of Rules: Devolution, Evolution, and Realism." *Wake Forest Law Review* 31 (1996): 693.

Wilson, James Q. *Bureaucracy: What Government Agencies Do and Why They Do It.* New York: Basic Books, 1989.

Wilson, James Q. *The Politics of Regulation.* New York: Basic Books, 1980.

Wood, Dan and Richard W. Waterman. "The Dynamics of Political Bureaucratic Adaptation." *American Journal of Political Science* 37 (1993): 497–528.

———. "The Dynamics of Political Control of the Bureaucracy." *American Political Science Review* 85 (1991): 801–828.

Woods, Neal D. "Interest Group Influence on State Administrative Rulemaking: The Impact of Rule Review." *The American Review of Public Administration* 35 (2005): 402–13.

———. "Political Influence on Agency Rule Making: Examining the Effects of Legislative and Gubernatorial Rule Review Powers." *State and Local Government Review* 36 (2004): 174–85.

Yackee, Jason Webb, and Susan Webb Yackee. "Administrative Procedures and Bureaucratic Performance: Is Federal Rule-Making Ossified?" *Journal of Public Administration Research and Theory* 20 (2010): 261.

———. "A Bias towards Business? Assessing Interest Group Influence on the U.S. Bureaucracy." *The Journal of Politics* 68 (2006): 128–39.

Yackee, Susan Webb. "Sweet-Talking the Fourth Branch: The Influence of Interest Group Comments on Federal Agency Rulemaking." *Journal of Public Administration Research and Theory* 16 (2006): 103–24.

Yohe, Gary W. "The Backward Incidence of Pollution Control-Some Comparative Statics in General Equilibrium." *Journal of Environmental Economics and Management* 6 (1979): 187–98.

Zambito, David Pascal. "An IRRC-Some Issue: Does Pennsylvania's Regulatory Review Act Violate the Separation of Powers." *Dickinson Law Review* 101 (1997): 643.

Index

For Product Safety Concerns and Information please contact our EU
representative GPSR@taylorandfrancis.com
Taylor & Francis Verlag GmbH, Kaufingerstraße 24, 80331 München, Germany

www.ingramcontent.com/pod-product-compliance
Lightning Source LLC
Chambersburg PA
CBHW062032270326
41929CB00014B/2407

9 781138 944718